AIDS IN DEVELOPING COUNTRIES

Nancy Harris, *Book Editor*

Daniel Leone, *President*
Bonnie Szumski, *Publisher*
Scott Barbour, *Managing Editor*
Helen Cothran, *Senior Editor*

GREENHAVEN
PRESS®

San Diego • Detroit • New York • San Francisco • Cleveland
New Haven, Conn. • Waterville, Maine • London • Munich

LIBRARY OF CONGRESS CATALOGING-IN-PUBLICATION DATA

AIDS in developing countries / Nancy Harris, book editor.
   p. cm. — (At issue)
Includes bibliographical references and index.
ISBN 0-7377-1789-0 (lib. bdg. : alk. paper) —
ISBN 0-7377-1790-4 (pbk. : alk. paper)
   1. AIDS (Disease)—Developing countries. I. Harris, Nancy 1952– . II. At issue
(San Diego, Calif.)
RA643.86.D44A337 2003
362.1'969792'0091724—dc21   2003042399

Printed in the United States of America

Contents

Introduction

During the twenty-year AIDS epidemic, almost twenty-two million people worldwide have died of the disease and an estimated 36 million are living with the HIV virus, which develops into AIDS. The first reported cases of HIV/AIDS in the early 1980s were followed, especially in the West, by rapid scientific advances in naming the disease, finding its cause, and learning about its modes of transmission. This burst of scientific discovery fostered an optimism that AIDS could be conquered. However, by the mid-1980s, the disease was recognized as an international epidemic. It spread explosively across the African continent and to many other parts of the world, including Asia and South America. It is estimated that 90 to 95 percent of AIDS infections occur in developing countries, primarily in sub-Saharan Africa where some of the world's worst living conditions exist. According to current estimates, 70 percent of those infected with AIDS live in this region. Today, AIDS is called pandemic because it has spread to every inhabited continent in the world.

Globally, AIDS is a disease which has been, and continues to be, primarily a sexually transmitted disease (STD) spread through unprotected sex between heterosexual men and women. It is shortening the life expectancy of working-age adults, dramatically increasing the number of infant and child deaths, shrinking the workforce, creating millions of orphans, widening the gap between rich and poor countries, and reversing developmental gains. Currently, the areas most affected by AIDS are Africa, India, and China. Almost every country in Asia and the Pacific area has recently experienced an increase in HIV infections.

Why AIDS is a major problem in developing countries

Wealthier countries have experienced a decrease in AIDS infections due partly to the development of AIDS medicines and the implementation of preventive measures. Government officials, medical scientists, and the public in Western countries have addressed many of the complex issues involved in combating AIDS. While the affluence of developed nations has helped decrease the transmission rates of AIDS in the West, widespread and worsening poverty in developing nations has limited public education about AIDS and the ability to act constructively to combat the disease. Poverty in developing countries has also blocked the development of adequate health care facilities and the purchase of AIDS medicines, even at drastically reduced prices. One estimate of the cost for AIDS drugs for an individual is $12,000 or more per year; however, the entire annual health budget of some African countries allots less than six dollars per person per year.

Although over 90 percent of people with AIDS live in developing countries, it is estimated that 90 percent of the AIDS drugs are consumed by those in the developed world. Large drug companies have not been interested in marketing AIDS drugs to poor countries because these countries have low purchasing power. A heated dispute arose in 1999 between the South African government and its supporters on one side and western pharmaceutical companies, the government of the United States, and the European Union on the other. The South African government attempted to reduce high drug costs by introducing amendments to international drug patent laws, but Western pharmaceutical companies reacted furiously, raising a lawsuit against forty South Africa–based drug companies. The western pharmaceutical companies argued that even if they did provide AIDS drugs more cheaply to developing countries, such nations had no infrastructure to administer the drugs. AIDS activists accused the pharmaceutical companies of putting profits before humanity. The issue was settled when the companies, pressured by worldwide public outrage, dropped their charges against the South African drug companies.

Poverty in developing nations not only blocks access to affordable AIDS medications, it also helps contribute to the spread of the disease. For example, evidence suggests that poor groups in developing countries, including injecting drug users and increasing numbers of commercial sex workers, run a higher risk of contracting AIDS. Many prostitutes reside along long-haul truck routes. Male and female adolescents between the ages of fifteen and nineteen, whose parents cannot provide them with adequate food and clothing, frequent these truck stops to trade sex for money and gifts. In addition, when men cannot find jobs in their villages, they go to bigger cities where they must work for months at a time. The men visit brothels and carry the AIDS infection back to their homes, often infecting their wives; in these countries, women are not expected to question their husbands or suggest the use of condoms. This same situation exists among businessmen, among whom it is not uncommon or socially unacceptable to have a wife and family as well as multiple sexual partners.

In addition to these problems, weak educational systems and lack of information about HIV/AIDS contribute to the spread of the disease. Some of those in developing countries do not know that they are infected with AIDS or even what the disease is. Embarrassment about having contracted AIDS as well as discrimination against those who have it can lead to an unhealthy silence and denial. Some governmental leaders in developing nations have not wanted to admit that their country has an AIDS problem. For example, Thabo Mbeki, the deputy president of South Africa, publicly stated that HIV and AIDS were not related issues. Some of these nations also suffer from internal strife, political upheaval, and wars, creating populations of refugees in which AIDS spreads unchecked. Other STD's and major diseases such as malaria and tuberculosis ravage some of these countries as well, complicating health care problems. Illnesses and deaths among people in their prime working years further impoverish these nations by hurting already weak economies and creating a new generation of "AIDS orphans," estimated at over eleven million children globally. Clearly, AIDS in developing countries is more than a health issue, as it undermines countries economically by affecting productivity, security, education, health care, civil service systems, social cohesion, and political stability.

What's being done to address the problem of AIDS

In response to the magnitude of the AIDS crisis, countries throughout the world have developed national AIDS programs (NAPs) adapted to the specific needs of their populations. The World Health Organization (WHO), a United Nations agency, founded a global HIV/AIDS trust fund in 1987 to help fund the NAP programs. These programs focus on the prevention of the sexual transmission of HIV and the transmission of HIV through blood and blood products, including injection drug use. The NAP programs have also supported strong international efforts to de-stigmatize AIDS and to ensure the human rights of those with HIV/AIDS. In addition, the programs attempt to reduce mother-to-child transmissions, which are a much greater issue in less affluent countries.

These national programs sometimes include working in partnerships with nongovernmental organizations (NGOs). NGOs, at the national level, provide a broad range of services, from confidential counseling and testing to support and legal services for people with AIDS. Some NGOs focus on solidarity, bringing people with AIDS together to fight the disease. Organizations composed of people living with HIV/AIDS are extensive and do international advocacy work to deal with the AIDS epidemic. One such organization, the Global Network of People Living with AIDS (GNP+), encourages members to network and share personal experiences. The organization leads the movement working to establish AIDS self-help groups. NGOs such as Doctors Without Borders, Oxfam, and The AIDS Coalition to Unleash Power have pressed drug companies to reduce their prices to poor countries. These activists are working to get generic versions of AIDS drugs at drastically reduced prices to countries in need.

Worldwide organizations have brought attention and resources to the global response to AIDS. The International AIDS Conference, which first convened in April 1985 in Atlanta, Georgia, has been the primary venue for professionals to share scientific and medical advances in AIDS research, as well as a forum for important AIDS policy debates. In addition, the United Nations established the joint UN Programme on HIV/AIDS (UNAIDS) to work with national governments and others to alleviate the AIDS epidemic. For example, in 1997, the UN gave China a 1.8 million dollar grant to help fight AIDS over a four year period. China used the funds to train ministry workers and increase prevention education among high-risk populations. HIV education programs are common in urban areas of China, but they have not reached rural areas. Another organization, the International HIV/AIDS Alliance, founded in 1993 in London, England, focuses its efforts in Africa, South America, and Asia, working to build up local AIDS organizations in these areas.

One of the few success stories in the fight against AIDS is Thailand, where the use of condoms is mandatory in brothels, which are closed down if they do not comply with government regulations. Thailand is one of the two developing nations, along with Uganda, which has experienced a drop in HIV infection rates and is a prime example of how prevention practices can work. In eastern Africa, where the rates of new infections are also beginning to stabilize or even decline, Uganda was the first country to report its AIDS cases. In the 1980s this country had the world's highest HIV infection rates, but the government responded quickly. After prevention through education and the promotion of safe-sex practices such as the use of condoms, Uganda has also experienced a decline in HIV rates.

Although some prevention efforts have succeeded, many analysts believe that the ultimate solution to the global AIDS crisis is the development of a vaccine that will prevent people from contracting AIDS in the first place. Many researchers believe that the development of a preventive vaccine is possible and absolutely necessary in order to eradicate AIDS. However, many pharmaceutical companies do not want to invest in AIDS vaccine research because of the large expense involved and the belief that profits could not be made on the vaccines. Funding for research to develop an AIDS vaccine comes from several sources, mainly the International AIDS Vaccine Initiative (IAVI), UNAIDS, the U.S. National Institutes of Health (NIH), U.S. government agencies, and a few multinational pharmaceutical companies. In 1997 U.S. President Bill Clinton called for the development of an HIV vaccine within a decade and announced a new center for vaccine research. Some researchers believe that a vaccine will be developed in the next five to seven years.

In the meantime, AIDS continues to spread in the developing world. Although successes have occurred, many experts contend that much more needs to be done. They argue that the response to AIDS needs to be of greater duration, greater quality, and greater scope to reach the many areas of life which AIDS touches and affects. Working together with others in the international community utilizing multiple approaches will enhance the ability of developing nations to cope with the disease. The viewpoints in *AIDS in Developing Countries: At Issue* explore the HIV/AIDS pandemic which has become an ongoing challenge to human ingenuity and compassion.

1

AIDS in Developing Countries: An Overview

United States Department of State

The United States Department of State is the leading foreign affairs agency of the United States government. The department formulates, represents, and implements the president's foreign policy.

AIDS statistics from 1999 reveal a grim situation in many of the world's developing countries. More than 95 percent of people with HIV/AIDS live in the developing world, and AIDS infections in developing countries are increasing. Many of these are in sub-Saharan Africa, but the trend is shifting to Asia where, along with some countries in the Pacific region, the AIDS virus is spreading swiftly. India is currently the nation with the greatest number of HIV/AIDS–infected individuals. The disease is also spreading in China, in parts of Latin America and Eastern Europe, and in Russia. The spread of AIDS in developing nations has hit children hard: The AIDS virus has orphaned over 1 million children and is expected to double infant and child mortality rates.

HIV/AIDS is insinuating itself into communities previously little troubled by the epidemic and is strengthening its grip on areas where AIDS is already the leading cause of death in adults. The cumulative number of those infected has more than tripled from the 10 million infections estimated in 1990. United Nations AIDS Program (UNAIDS) and the World Health Organization estimate that more than 33 million people are infected with HIV and that 16,000 new infections are acquired every day. Worldwide, an estimated 13.9 million people have lost their lives to the disease—2.5 million in 1998 alone. Given the current rate of infection as well as the sheer number of those already infected and the limited availability of state of the art care, the death toll from HIV/AIDS is projected to increase exponentially in the years to come.

HIV/AIDS is a global problem touching virtually every country and every family around the world. It does not recognize boundaries of nationality, gender, age, occupation or sexual preference. Globally, 1 in

United States Department of State, "Introduction: World AIDS Situation," *U.S. International Response to HIV/AIDS*, 1999.

every 100 adults 15 to 49 years of age is HIV-infected; at least 80 percent of these infections are due to heterosexual transmission.

Where AIDS has spread

HIV/AIDS is resident in humans in every region of the globe, from sub-Saharan Africa to Asia and the Pacific, the Americas, Eastern and Western Europe, to the Middle East. However, HIV infections are concentrated largely in countries least able to afford the care for infected people. In fact, more than 95 percent of people with HIV live in the developing world. It is estimated that by the year 2020 HIV will be responsible for 37 percent of all adult deaths from infectious diseases in the developing world.

HIV/AIDS is a global problem touching virtually every country and every family around the world.

HIV/AIDS is now threatening development gains that local and donor governments, citizens, nongovernmental organizations, and international agencies have worked for decades to achieve. In many sub-Saharan African countries, AIDS has increased infant mortality and reduced life expectancy to levels not seen since the 1960s. Infant and child mortality rates are expected to double and even triple early in the [twenty-first] century. By the year 2010, life expectancy in some sub-Saharan countries could decrease by 30 years or more. AIDS is doubling, or even tripling, death rates among young adults in countries in southern Africa. In Botswana and Zimbabwe, prevalence among young adults has reached 25 percent—one person in four, a historic new high. In South Africa, it is estimated that 3 million people are now living with HIV, and 700,000 were infected in 1997 alone. Deputy President [Thabo] Mbeki, speaking for President [Nelson] Mandela, has stated that South African economic growth could slow by 1 percent a year because of AIDS.

Children with AIDS

Globally, the number of children under 15 who have lived with or are living with HIV/AIDS since the start of the epidemic in the late 1970s has reached approximately 3.8 million—2.7 million of whom have already died. Nearly 600,000 children were infected with HIV in 1998; most were infected before or during birth or through breastfeeding by HIV-infected mothers. From the beginning of the epidemic until the start of 1998, some 8.2 million children around the world lost their mothers to AIDS. In 1997, it is estimated that HIV/AIDS orphaned 1.6 million children. At present, 90 percent of the orphans live in sub-Saharan Africa.

The shifting problem

An important trend of the 1990s has been the beginning of a shift of the global AIDS problem from Africa to Asia, which will soon have more new HIV infections than any other region of the world. The recent spread of the HIV epidemic in Asia and the Pacific has been swift. Since 1994, almost every country in Asia and the Pacific region has seen HIV prevalence rates increase by more than 100 percent. Nearly 7.2 million people in the region are now believed to be living with HIV. In years to come, that number may grow dramatically. India and China, the two most populous countries on earth, have experienced exponential growth. India, with a population of over 900 million, had 3–5 million people infected [from 1996 to 1998], making it currently the nation with the greatest number of HIV/AIDS-infected individuals. China, the world's most populous nation, will need to act quickly and effectively to avoid following a similar course.

In some countries—such as Indonesia and the Philippines—HIV has remained at roughly the same low levels for a number of years. The situation in Latin America is mixed, with prevalence rising rapidly in Mexico, Brazil and Guyana. In other countries, as in many industrialized nations, infection rates have stabilized or are falling. The level of damage sustained by developing nations varies with the maturity of the epidemic and the response of national authorities and local communities to the threat of its spread throughout the population.

In Eastern Europe, though the absolute numbers are lower, many countries have experienced a doubling or tripling of their infections since 1994. Before 1995, the incidence of HIV/AIDS in the former Soviet Union and Eastern Europe was negligible. However, in 1996, 8,000 new HIV cases were reported. The bulk of the spread has been in injecting drug users and the sex partners of injecting drug users (IDU), which may provide a bridge for the virus into the general population. In Russia 2,223 cases of HIV were reported in the first 6 months of 1997, and by the year 2000, without appropriate interventions to eliminate illegal injection drug use and to curb high-risk behaviors, as many as 1 million Russians could be infected with HIV.

The long lag time between HIV infection, development of AIDS symptoms, and death—which is 4–5 years in developing countries and 10 years, on average, in industrialized countries—helps explain why most countries have yet to see the damage the epidemic can do to their social and economic fabric.

2

AIDS Is a Threat to Human Development and Security in Developing Countries

Fiona Young

Fiona Young is a writer for the UN Chronicle, *a quarterly publication of the United Nations that has covered the organization's activities and events since its inception.*

AIDS is not only a health issue but involves human development and security issues as well, especially in developing countries. As recently as 1998 the AIDS epidemic was handled solely as a health problem, but presently, all bodies of the United Nations are giving the disease much broader attention. Situations in various countries exemplify the connection between AIDS and economic development, such as in Thailand, where farm output and income fell 52 percent because of the numbers of farmers who died from AIDS. In the Ivory Coast seven teachers a week die from AIDS, illustrating the devastating effect AIDS has on human development. AIDS also threatens human security. For example, female refugees are often infected with AIDS as a result of forced sex or sex traded for food and other necessities.

Ten years ago, a handful of health professionals and community leaders like Elhadj Sy asked, prodded and cajoled governments and ministers to pay attention to a disease called HIV/AIDS (human immunodeficiency virus/acquired immune deficiency syndrome).

"HIV/AIDS was impacting development", said Mr. Sy, the Joint United Nations Programme on HIV/AIDS (UNAIDS) Representative in New York and whose work on the disease began in the eighties. "But there were many people, many government officials who didn't think so. One minister of health told me 'we can discuss malaria but not this AIDS of yours'".

Ten years later, as the number of global infections hit 36.1 million, the HIV/AIDS battle is gaining momentum. On three occasions in 2000, the United Nations Security Council discussed HIV/AIDS. The story of HIV/AIDS when addressed as a health problem offers vastly different endings compared to when it is addressed as a human security threat.

When government leaders take action

Take the example of Senegal. In 1986, when the first six cases of HIV/AIDS were reported, the government responded immediately and created a national AIDS programme. By 1987, blood transfusions were systematically scanned in ten regions of the country. By 1992, awareness of the disease had become part of primary school curriculums. Soccer games included messages about HIV/AIDS on stadium banners and on t-shirts of players. Young people mobilized to fight the disease, "even though they had never seen a person living with AIDS", recalled Mr. Sy. The government incorporated HIV/AIDS across development policies, and today Senegal boasts one of the lowest HIV/AIDS rates in Africa—1.77 per cent.

In Brazil, President Fernando Cardoso, in a 1996 Presidential Decree, recommitted providing universal access to HIV/AIDS antiviral therapies under his country's public health care system. "The health authorities in Brazil determined that the cost of the spread of AIDS in Brazil would be extremely high", said Ambassador Gelson Fonseca, Jr., Brazil's Permanent Representative to the United Nations. "They determined it was better to spend money on prevention, because it will save money in the long run". By 2001, Brazil's national AIDS policy decreased the numbers of HIV/AIDS-related deaths by 50 per cent and of hospitalizations by 75 per cent.

In 1992, when the Uganda AIDS Commission began coordinating their national HIV/AIDS strategy, the Government faced a 14 per cent infection rate. By December 2000, the rate decreased to 8.3 percent.

The story of HIV/AIDS when addressed as a health problem offers vastly different endings compared to when it is addressed as a human security threat.

And the list goes on. When top leaders pay attention, changes can happen.

Look at the United Nations. "Even in 1998, AIDS was still very much seen as a health disease to be dealt with in a health forum, not as a social development problem", said David Lawson, a Liaison Officer for UNAIDS in New York. But today, beyond the seven co-sponsoring bodies of UN-AIDS—the UN Children's Fund, the UN Development Programme, the UN Population Fund, the UN Educational, Scientific and Cultural Organization, the UN Office for Drug Control and Crime Prevention, the World Health Organization (WHO) and the World Bank—every UN body addresses HIV/AIDS.

When the United States first pushed to have HIV/AIDS discussed in the Security Council, many nations protested for procedural reasons. "They felt that the Security Council was not the appropriate venue for social and economic issues", said Mr. Lawson. But the United States persisted. "Unless we act effectively and decisively now, HIV/AIDS might be the worst pandemic we have ever seen", said former United States Vice-President Al Gore, who presided over the Council's first meeting on HIV/AIDS. "Absolutely the United States should address HIV/AIDS as a national security issue", he said in a recent interview with the Chronicle. "AIDS is a security issue, just as the environment is a security issue".

Results of the first Security Council meeting

Two results emerged from the Council's first meeting in January 2000 on the "impact of AIDS on peace and security in Africa". First, national governments increased funding. The United States pledged a total of $300 million per year; Canada increased funding to address HIV in Africa by $50 million; the United Kingdom pledged an additional $38 million; Australia, $10 million over the next four years; Italy, $20 million to international partnerships working with AIDS in Africa; Norway, an additional $3.6 million; and the Netherlands pledged an additional $1.5 million.

Economic development and physical, social and human capital erode as HIV/AIDS prevalence rates rise.

Second, Ambassador Volodymyer Yu. Yel'chenko, Ukraine's Permanent Representative, floated the idea of a General Assembly special session on HIV/AIDS in his remarks to the Council. "It is high time for the United Nations to update a comprehensive agenda for action against this pandemic. In this connection, it might be appropriate that the Security Council use its prerogatives and recommend to the General Assembly that it convene a special session to consider new strategies, methods, practical activities and specific measures to strengthen international cooperation in addressing this problem".

Further persistence by a coalition of Member States, spearheaded by Ukraine, led to Assembly resolution 55/13. From 25 to 27 June [2000], Member States, civil society representatives and individuals living with HIV/AIDS reviewed the problem of HIV/AIDS in all its aspects.

The first resolution on a health issue

In July 2000, the Security Council met again—this time to discuss UN peacekeeping operations and their impact on HIV/AIDS—unanimously adopting its first resolution (1308(2000)) on a health issue. "The draft resolution that the Council is considering is historic", said Dr. Peter Piot, Executive Director of UNAIDS. "It would be the first recognition in this body and by the international community of a link between AIDS—an infection—and human security and development". In a follow-up meeting in January 2001, the Council renewed political commitment. While it did not resolve to revisit the issue, "you can guess that if the Security Council discussed AIDS three times in a year, they may address it in the future if need be", said Mr. Lawson.

While the role of, and dangers to, peacekeeping forces in the HIV/

AIDS crisis is only one leaf on a complex tree, the impact of the Council's discussions in mobilizing top leadership is undisputed. "It was important for the Security Council to address HIV/AIDS to increase global awareness", said Ambassador Fonseca. "But AIDS in itself is not a security issue. It could affect the social fabric by weakening the capacity of the State, but I don't know if we have reached that state yet".

HIV/AIDS poses a security threat in one area that receives scarce attention: women, children, refugees and internally displaced persons caught in emergency settings.

"I have seen AIDS as a human security threat", says Mr. Sy. "I have seen fields without crops, communities without adults, communities where the main weekend activity is going to funerals, organized together so they don't have to go to funerals everyday". In Thailand, farm output and income fell 52 per cent among rural families affected by HIV/AIDS. In the Ivory Coast, seven teachers a week die as a result of HIV/AIDS. In Botswana, average life expectancy without AIDS was 69 years. Today, with over one third of the population infected with the disease, average life expectancy is 44 years.

In India, 3.7 million people were estimated to be living with HIV/AIDS at the beginning of the millennium—more than any other country, bar South Africa. Only 5 per cent of cases are estimated to be reported in China, and the Russian Federation registered 50,000 new infections in 2000—a number more than the previous 10 years combined.

A 2000 World Bank study estimates that Zimbabwe and Zambia will see a 30-per-cent drop in gross domestic product (GDP) over the next 10 years due to HIV/AIDS. And most infected people do not know they are HIV-positive. René Bonnel, lead Economist for the AIDS Campaign Team for Africa at the World Bank, says HIV/AIDS is a long-term economic problem. His recent report found the economic costs of AIDS staggering.

"In a typical sub-Saharan country, with a prevalence rate of 20 per cent, the rate of growth of GDP would be 2.6 percentage points less each year. At the end of a 20-year period, GDP would be 67 per cent less than otherwise". He also notes a recent change in attitude as leaders see the effects of AIDS. Children run households and fathers can no longer teach their sons how to grow crops. Economic development and physical, social and human capital erode as HIV/AIDS prevalence rates rise.

Incentives to train workers or send children to school diminish as shorter life expectancies due to HIV/AIDS reduce the rate of return on human capital investments. It kills managers, teachers, mothers and fathers in their most productive years. "One year ago there was a division between people working in the health field and staff in the Ministry of Finance. The Staff at the Ministry of Finance felt that HIV/AIDS was a health problem, not a problem of the highest level", recalled Mr. Bonnel. "In September 1999, no government would raise HIV/AIDS with the World Bank during annual country meetings. Now, most governments raise the issue of HIV/AIDS themselves".

Although the Security Council has addressed AIDS, and the Secretary-General has called HIV/AIDS his personal priority, some governments still resist decisively addressing AIDS. Some governments, according to Mr. Sy, still want to present themselves to the world as a clean nation. He added: "AIDS is about sex and blood and procreation. Because it affects everyone, it wakes up many fears and apprehensions at the individual level. If you're talking to a government official who has had many sexual partners and has his own fears, he may repress or deny his own fears before taking on AIDS, as a minister or social servant".

AIDS in emergency situations

Finally, HIV/AIDS poses a security threat in one area that receives scarce attention: women, children, refugees and internally displaced persons caught in emergency settings. Assistance in emergency settings among vulnerable populations was largely ignored until last year, according to Dr. Lianne Kuppens, a WHO medical doctor who is the Desk Officer for Africa, Indonesia and East Timor, as well as WHO's focal person for HIV/AIDS in Complex Emergencies.

Women in particular find themselves at higher risk of HIV/AIDS infection. While the numbers remain unclear, during the Rwanda and Sierra Leone conflicts the infection rates increased due to rape and "survival sex", where women who were desperate to gain access to food, shelter or water traded sex for necessities.

In emergency situations, a country's first priority is not HIV/AIDS. Health infrastructures and HIV/AIDS sentinel surveillance systems collapse. "Even those that deal with HIV/AIDS professionally cannot in a conflict situation", said Dr. Kuppens. "No one is addressing this in a coordinated way". Providing condoms, a safe blood supply and health education materials can make a difference in acute emergency settings, but resources remain a problem. "I don't see any funds going to HIV/AIDS in conflict situations", said Dr. Kuppens. "We need to add funding for HIV/AIDS and vulnerable populations in complex emergencies".

Maybe, when world leaders consider HIV/AIDS in emergency settings as an urgent human security threat will those women, children, refugees and internally displaced persons at risk of contracting it have stories with healthier endings.

3

The United States Should Provide Financial Assistance to Developing Countries to Combat AIDS

David Gergen

David Gergen is editor at large of U.S. News & World Report *and an analyst on ABC's* Nightline. *He is a professor of public service at the John F. Kennedy School of Government and directs its Center for Public Leadership. Gergen has served as an adviser to four presidents, the latest of whom was former president Bill Clinton. Under Clinton, he served as counselor on foreign policy and domestic affairs and then as special international adviser.*

The United States has a moral and financial obligation to help less fortunate countries fight AIDS. These poor countries cannot overcome the disease alone. Africa has the highest AIDS mortality rate and is in critical need of help, as exemplified by the country of Botswana, where an estimated 70 percent of teenagers are expected to die of the disease. Although the global AIDS epidemic has persisted for two decades, wealthy nations are only now starting to seriously assist less developed countries.

A half century ago, the world plunged into the worst catastrophe in all of history as nations from every continent sent their soldiers into battle. Over 16 million combatants lost their lives in World War II, casting a terrible pall over the human experience. Today, the people of Africa are fighting an even deadlier war. Over 17 million souls have perished so far—and who cares?

The struggle against AIDS and related diseases in Africa poses one of the greatest moral tests of our time. Will the advanced nations of the world choose to act on behalf of people who cannot win this fight on their own, or will they look away? For two decades, we have shilly-shallied, per-

David Gergen, "A Moment to Step Up," *U.S. News & World Report*, vol. 130, February 26, 2001, p. 72. Copyright © 2001 by U.S. News & World Report, Inc. Reproduced by permission.

haps because many of us thought that the problem was so big and intractable that it defied solution. But that excuse is now unacceptable. A coalition of doctors, public health officials, economists, and others are finally developing a promising plan of attack by wealthy nations that, for a relatively small cost, could relieve massive suffering and begin bringing the spread of AIDS under control. Their ideas deserve urgent attention.

The struggle against AIDS and related diseases in Africa poses one of the greatest moral tests of our time.

They grow out of recent, encouraging trends in the prices of anti-AIDS cocktails. For some time, it has been possible for HIV/AIDS patients in the United States to take drug combinations that help them live longer, richer lives. But the price is steep. In the United States, drug companies typically charge $10,000 to $15,000 per patient per year.

Now, though, prices are falling—dramatically. Some pharmaceutical companies have been lowering the price to $1,000 per patient in the developing world. [In February 2001] a generic-drug manufacturer in India, Cipla, announced that it would sell an AIDS cocktail for $600 to low-income governments and for $350 annually to Doctors Without Borders, one of the finest nonprofits in the world.

Rich nations negotiate the cost of AIDS drugs

Seizing upon those breakthroughs, health officials and scholars recently gathered at a retrovirus conference in Chicago and then at Harvard to map out a blueprint for treating people in the African nations most afflicted. Their plan calls for rich nations to negotiate the costs of drug cocktails down to at most $500 per patient per year, to choose two African countries and a number of smaller projects as models, and to integrate AIDS treatment with tuberculosis-control programs. Harvard's Jeffrey Sachs, an indefatigable force in trying to help poor countries pick themselves up, has taken to the newspapers here and abroad to promote the effort. He estimates that the overall cost for wealthy nations would run between $10 billion and $20 billion a year, of which the U.S. tab would be around $3 billion. That would represent about $10 a year for every American—"the cost of a movie ticket with popcorn."

It is obvious that desperate African nations cannot cope on their own. Many of these societies are collapsing. In the southern cone, at least 1 in 5 adults is infected. In Zambia, teachers are dying as fast as they are being trained. In Zimbabwe and Botswana, as many as 70 percent of teenagers are expected to die. With average incomes of about $500 a year, and terror spreading, these countries are becoming human hellholes.

Commendably, national-security officials, including Secretary of State Colin Powell, have recognized that the unraveling in southern Africa presents national security concerns for the United States. The CIA frets that if the pandemic continues to spread, we could see massive numbers of refugees, further economic disruption, and a spread of civil war. In their nightmares, public-health officials worry that virulent strains of AIDS, common in Africa, and drug-resistant tuberculosis could spread to developed nations and introduce diseases that are virtually untreatable. Even if we could erect barriers to protect us, however, we would still face the moral question of what we owe others less fortunate. Some say forget about the Africans: They have been mired in troubles for thousands of years, and we need the money for our own. Frankly, the argument about cost rings hollow. The real issue is whether we will continue to be a generous and caring people, as we have been for most of our history. Generations of Europeans are still grateful for the blood and treasure we spent on their behalf during and just after World War II. True, the United States cannot become an international 911, but when the worst disease strikes since the bubonic plague, surely we will want our children to know that we stood up and did the right thing. Let's get moving.

4

The AIDS Epidemic Demands Action from the International Community

Colin L. Powell

Colin L. Powell is the United States Secretary of State. General Powell served in the Vietnam and Korean Wars and received numerous U.S. military decorations. In addition, Powell served as twelfth chairman of the Joint Chiefs of Staff, Department of Defense, from 1989 through 1993.

The current global response to HIV/AIDS is inadequate, especially considering that the causes of the devastating disease are known and prevention is possible. In order to fight the disease, people at all levels of society must combat taboos concerning AIDS and challenge the traditions that have enabled the disease to spread. The silence that has surrounded the AIDS issue and contributed to discrimination against those infected with AIDS must be broken. All sectors of society and governments worldwide must make a concerted effort and take immediate action against AIDS.

Ladies and gentlemen, the world has entered an age of immense promise. The spread of democracy and market economies, and breakthroughs in technology, permit us to envision a day in this century when most of humanity will be freed from tyranny and poverty.

Yet, we have been blind to the fact that this promising new century has arrived at a time of plague. It is twenty years since the onset of the HIV/AIDS crisis, but we have only just begun to grasp the threat it poses to this promising new world.

AIDS is often likened to the Bubonic plague of the 14th century, which killed one-third of Europe. But this is not the Middle Ages, ladies and gentlemen. Back then, people did not know what caused the pestilence or how it spread. They thought that it resulted from an alignment of the planets, or was visited upon them for their sins by a wrathful God.

We of the 21st century know better. We know that a virus causes AIDS. And we know how to prevent its spread. Treatments have been developed. Science has given us grounds to hope for vaccines and, ultimately, for a cure.

Colin L. Powell, "U.N. Special Session on HIV/AIDS: Silence Kills," *Vital Speeches of the Day*, vol. LXVII, July 15, 2001, pp. 578–80.

All this is known. Yet, to date, our global response to this rapidly spreading scourge has been woefully inadequate. What will historians say of us if we continue to delay? Will history record a fateful moment in our time, on our watch, when action came too late?

AIDS respects no man, woman or child. It knows no race, religion, class or creed. No community, country, or continent is immune from its ravages. Let us resolve that, from this moment on, our response to AIDS must be no less comprehensive, no less relentless and no less swift than the pandemic itself.

President [George W.] Bush joins Secretary General [Kofi] Annan in the conviction that AIDS is so immense in its scope and profound in its impact that it compels new thinking and concerted action. As the President has said: "Only through sustained and focused international cooperation can we address problems so grave and suffering so great."

Last month [July 2001] President Bush announced a pledge of $200 million to jump start the global fund, a bold, new public/private partnership to combat HIV/AIDS, tuberculosis and malaria. We hope this seed money will help generate billions more from donors all over the world. And more will come from the United States as we learn where our support can be most effective.

Beyond the global fund, I am proud to say that my government has been, and will continue to be, the largest bilateral donor in the fight against AIDS, providing 50 percent of all international funding. To date, the United States has dedicated over $1.6 billion to combat AIDS in the developing world. President Bush's budget for the next fiscal year seeks $480 million, more than double the fiscal year 2000 amount. The President is also requesting over $3.4 billion for AIDS research. The United States—I pledge today—will continue to lead the world in funding vital research.

President Bush has put the full force of his government, the full force of his cabinet, behind the U.S. response to this crisis. He has named Secretary of Health and Human Services Tommy Thompson, who is here today, and me to co-chair a special task force to ensure that my government's efforts are comprehensive and coordinated.

Comprehensive and coordinated these efforts must be, for AIDS is not just a humanitarian or health issue. It not only kills. It also destroys communities. It decimates countries. It destabilizes regions. It can consume continents. No war on the face of the earth is more destructive than the AIDS pandemic.

I was a soldier. But I know of no enemy in war more insidious or vicious than AIDS, an enemy that poses a clear and present danger to the world. The war against AIDS has no front lines. We must wage it on every front. And only an integrated approach makes sense. An approach that emphasizes prevention and public education. But it also must include treatment, care for orphans, measures to stop mother-to-child transmission, affordable drugs, delivery systems and infrastructure, medical training. And of course, it must include research into vaccines and a cure.

All of these elements are essential and must be aggressively pursued. But unless a strong emphasis is put on prevention, prevention and more prevention, this pandemic will continue to rage out of control.

In this global war against AIDS, everyone can and must be a leader. Everyone can and must be an ally. We are all vulnerable—big nations and small, the wealthy and the poor. We cannot let AIDS divide us. My country is ready to work with all nations to build a global coalition of action against this common foe.

It is not just governments who can play leadership roles. Philanthropists, foundations and corporations must step up to the challenge. Contributing to the global fund is one important way to do that, and I urge all the members of the international community, public and private, to join in making substantial pledges to this crusade.

I do not, however, want to leave the impression that the global fund is only for big donors. United Nations International Children's Emergency Fund (UNICEF) is a wonderful example of how grassroots efforts can raise significant money and international awareness.

Leadership also comes from individuals, non-governmental institutions and faith-based organizations. Let me describe just a few of those kinds of organizations that are doing such wonderful work, people who are doing such wonderful work, the kind of people and organizations we can help with this trust fund.

For example, there is Dr. Jean William Pape, who co-founded the only institution in Haiti that gives post-graduate AIDS training to medical workers. Or in Poland, Father Arkadiusz Nowak speaks out against the misperception that AIDS is a punishment from God. He has established a foundation and homes for people with AIDS. In Tahiti, twenty-six-year-old journalist Maire Bopp Dupont has used her HIV-positive status to raise awareness through a popular radio show.

All of these people doing what they can, speaking out. And we should help encourage millions more to do so.

Silence kills. Silence kills. Breaking the silence is a powerful way that people at all levels of society can combat the disease. I do not minimize the courage it can take to come forward, to challenge taboos and change traditions. But that kind of courage is needed or more people will die. Opinion leaders from all walks of life must deliver the message that AIDS is real. That our enemy is the HIV virus, not its victims. That those who carry HIV deserve compassion, not ostracism. That they deserve to be treated with dignity, not with disdain. I must, you must, all public officials must use the spotlight we are given to speak out and make AIDS a top priority.

Many speakers have noted the dreadful toll that AIDS is taking. And after the tenth or the twentieth speech, even the most shocking statistics start to numb. But let me try to make it more relevant.

This hall holds about 2,000 people. By the time three hours of this session elapse, 2,000 people around the world—just about the same number who are here—will be newly infected with HIV/AIDS. That's one for every one in this room.

In some countries the infection rate is so high that one in three of us—the delegate to your right, the delegate to your left, or you, yourself— would be HIV positive. If this disease goes unchecked, the misery and the destruction will continue to grow exponentially. It can rob us all of our future. We must not let it rob us of our future.

The world is looking to us today. The world wants us to act. We must act, and we must act now. This is the time. This is the place. And we must not fail the people of the world who are looking to us for leadership. Thank you very much.

5

The AIDS Epidemic Demands Action from Developing Countries

The Economist

The Economist is Britain's leading newsweekly.

It is not possible for others to solve the AIDS problem in developing nations. In Africa, for example, where the AIDS epidemic is most severe, Africans themselves need to be taking steps to help address the crisis. These steps include facing the fact that AIDS is mainly a sexually transmitted disease, relinquishing the taboos involved in talking about it, and encouraging the use of condoms. Another step is to test pregnant women for HIV and give them the appropriate anti-AIDS drugs, making certain to upgrade health care facilities to administer the drugs. In addition, women must be educated so that they can feel empowered to say no to unprotected sex. Money from the West cannot solve the AIDS problem in developing nations; those countries must help themselves.

It is hard to absorb the full reality. [As of July 2000] the global AIDS epidemic is thought to have killed 19 million people. That is almost twice as many as died in the first world war. It has infected another 34 million. When they die, as most will in the next few years, AIDS will have killed nearly as many as the second world war. And the epidemic shows no signs of abating. UNAIDS, the umbrella group that co-ordinates the anti-AIDS effort of various UN agencies, reckons that 5 million people a year are being infected with the human immunodeficiency virus (HIV) that causes AIDS. If these people were dying from bullets and bombs, they would never be out of the headlines.

Not for nothing is the slogan of the international AIDS conference that has taken place in Durban in 2000 "break the silence". Now that drugs can ward off the effects of AIDS in people who can afford them, the issue has slid out of sight in the rich world. Seen from that world, AIDS is just another disease, like malaria, measles and mumps, which westerners

The Economist, "The Battle with AIDS," *The Economist*, vol. 356, July 15, 2000, p. 17. Copyright © 2000 by The Economist Newspaper Group. Reproduced by permission.

can ignore in the knowledge that they are unlikely to catch it and will not die of it even if they do.

Yet AIDS is not just another infection, and comparing its victims with the casualty lists of a war is not mere rhetoric. Most diseases pick off young children and the elderly. AIDS hits those in the prime of life. The human disaster for its victims and their families thus feeds into a social and economic disaster for the countries affected. And, with few exceptions, those countries are in Africa, a continent that has dire enough economic and social problems already.

Helping those who help themselves

Attitudes are at last starting to change. In January [2000] the American government upgraded the threat of AIDS from one that merely affects people's health to one that affects the security of nations. James Wolfensohn, president of the World Bank, has declared that there is "no limit" to the amount the Bank will spend on AIDS, and it announced at the start of the conference that $500 million is now available. And in May [2000] five large drug companies agreed with UNAIDS not only that something must be done, but that they might help. One company, Merck, has put $50 million of its money where its mouth is. It plans to deliver, with the Gates Foundation, an American charity, what it claims will be a comprehensive anti-AIDS package for Botswana, the worst-affected country of all.

AIDS hits those in the prime of life. The human disaster for its victims and their families thus feeds into a social and economic disaster.

Such initiatives are welcome, even if they are a drop in the ocean (the World Bank estimates that Africa alone may need to spend $2.3 billion a year on the disease). But it is rarely possible for outsiders to solve other peoples' problems. AIDS in poor countries will not go away so long as their leaders do not give a lead in fighting against it. And Africa's rulers, with one or two shining exceptions, have not yet done so. Some have simply ignored the problem.

Sadly, South Africa, the conference's host, is a shining bad example. It makes angry noises at drug firms, while failing to promote the use of medicines such as azidothymidine (AZT) and nevirapine that are known to be effective at preventing the transmission of HIV from mother to child at birth. And Thabo Mbeki, the country's president, who has been listening to a small band of scientists with eccentric and discredited opinions, has allowed doubts to linger over whether AIDS is actually caused by HIV in the first place. Certainly, Africa has some special features. Africans are beset by many diseases, each of which serves to weaken people and to make them susceptible to the others. And poverty aggravates the problem, as do incessant wars. If Africa were as rich and peaceful as Europe or America, AIDS might by now be as rare there as elsewhere. But it is not, ultimately, a lack of money that causes AIDS. It is a virus. And stopping, or slowing, that virus is not impossible, as the example of Uganda, which has reduced its level of infection from 14% to 8% over the past decade, shows.

Steps that need to be taken

There are a few simple but important steps that need to be taken. The first is to stop being squeamish about sex. AIDS is mainly a sexually transmitted disease. That means that people enjoy giving it to each other. Talking about sex is taboo in many African cultures. But in places like Uganda, the taboo has been overcome. All successful prevention campaigns have worked by preaching ways, notably the use of condoms, that reduce the enjoyment of sex only slightly. Campaigns that have merely preached abstinence have always failed.

The second idea is to test pregnant women for HIV, and give them AZT or nevirapine if they turn out to be infected. This is a cheapish and effective use of anti-AIDS drugs, which ought to be near the top of even the poorest country's health budget. Health systems also must be better run so that the drugs are properly administered and followed up, to minimise the risk of the virus developing resistance. These steps, alone, could save 500,000 infant lives a year.

The other way to help stop the spread of AIDS is to empower women so that they can say no. This is terribly difficult in the many patriarchal—i.e., exploitative—African cultures. Yet women who are educated have a much better chance of saying no than women who are not. The no does not have to be no to all sex. But it does need to be no to unprotected sex with anybody about whose HIV status a woman is unsure. Men too would benefit from better education in the dangers and risks attached to AIDS, but education of girls is less often attempted and yet even more important, because they are more likely to act to slow the spread of the virus. So this must be a third plank of an effective anti-AIDS strategy.

Condoms. Healthy births. And educated women. These will not abolish AIDS. That, if it ever happens, will require effective vaccines, and those are years away. They might, however, contain it and stop the deaths of many of the young, vigorous people whom poor countries need. Africans, and indeed all people in poor countries where the disease has a grip, should be shouting out about these things. It is that shout that needs to break the silence. No amount of cheering from the sidelines by the West will do instead.

6

African Nations Are Committed to Fighting the AIDS Epidemic

Mary M. Kanya

Mary M. Kanya is the ambassador of Swaziland, one of the countries of southern Africa hardest hit by the AIDS epidemic.

Contrary to the common belief that Africans are in denial about the AIDS epidemic and are not making efforts to help themselves, African leaders are committed to addressing the AIDS crisis in sub-Saharan Africa. Southern Africa's efforts are evident in countries such as Zimbabwe, which has implemented a 3 percent tax to pay for AIDS health care costs, and also in Botswana, which is developing a national AIDS agency to fight the AIDS epidemic. In addition, the political leaders of the Southern African Development Community (SADC), made up of the five southern African countries most affected by AIDS, are developing coordinated national action plans focused on prevention, care, and support of people infected by AIDS. Furthermore, scientists in southern Africa are working on using AIDS drugs to prevent AIDS transmission from mother to child.

I n my submission I would like to dispel the misconception that African political leaders are not aware or committed to addressing the HIV/AIDS pandemic, that Africans are still in denial, and that the Africans are not helping themselves.

You have already heard about the progress that has been made in Uganda, Senegal, Zambia and other countries. These successes I am sure would not have come by if there was no political commitment.

The statistics [below] to us are not just figures. We see the negative impact that the epidemic is having on our society. We personally experience it. Those statistics represent people we know, the teacher, the banker, the engineer and the politician, who have to teach our young and move our economy and community forward. How can we deny it? How

Mary M. Kanya, Submission at a Hearing on the AIDS Crisis in Developing Countries and on Legislation Before the House Committee on Banking and Financial Services, March 8, 2000.

can we not care? What we do, we do within the very limited resources available to our countries, and to our people. It will take a long time though to see a reversal in the severity of the epidemic because all the causes that fuel the AIDS epidemic are not fully understood. At a Senate hearing on AIDS in Africa, The Honourable U.S. Surgeon General Dr. David Satcher was asked why the African continent, South of the Sahara, which accounts for only 10% of the world's population, carries the heaviest burden of the AIDS epidemic. His response was that the scientists don't know, they are still searching.

We have an African proverb which goes, "there is a poisonous snake in the house, and we need to find ways to get it out before it kills us!"

This does not just apply to us as Africans. This virus respects no borders, it travels easily throughout our global village. What one country does, impacts on many others.

What are African countries doing

Let me give you a glimpse of what some countries are doing either individually or as sub-regional groups. I am best able to speak about the Southern African Development Community (SADC) region where five countries with the Sub-Saharan Africa's highest HIV infection rates are, including my own country, Swaziland, where the population is 970,000:

- 22% of the population is HIV positive
- 80% of in patients in major hospitals are HIV positive
- 30% of pregnant women who attend pre-natal clinics test HIV positive
- About 60% HIV infections occur amongst those 20–39 years old
- Almost 18% of all University students are infected with HIV.

As a result of the above statistics, His Majesty King Mswati III of Swaziland, in opening Parliament in February 1999, declared HIV/AIDS a national disaster.

He further said, "The HIV/AIDS epidemic is an unacceptable situation, whose real effects will be felt only in the coming years as more and more of the economically active fall to the disease, and more and more medical effort and resources are diverted to treating the effects. I appeal once more to everyone to take warning and to understand that each and everyone of us is at risk. This is already a national disaster and requires a truly national effort to bring about a complete reversal in attitude and behaviour."

In Zimbabwe when the Minister of Finance presented his Budget Speech for 2000, he introduced a new tax . . . a 3% tax on money earned by individuals and corporations to pay for AIDS healthcare costs. I understand this has already been passed by Parliament.

In Botswana, a National AIDS Co-ordinating Agency is to be established in a bid to fight the HIV/AIDS pandemic. Presenting the 2000–2001 Budget Estimates in Parliament, the Minister of Finance and Development Planning said this multi-disciplinary agency, to be headed by a Permanent Secretary, would be reporting to the AIDS Council, which is chaired by the President. Among its tasks would be overseeing the implementation of the National Operation Plan developed in 1998.

- All the political leaders in SADC are fully committed to address the HIV/AIDS epidemic within the resources at their disposal.

• They are in the process of developing coordinated national action plans focussing on prevention, care and support of persons infected and affected by HIV/AIDS. Although it is culturally the norm that orphans are taken care of by the community, the extremely high numbers of orphans projected over the next few years will require that we consider alternatives such as children's homes supported through public-private contributions.

• Our scientists are looking at the use of drugs such as AZT [azidothymidine] and Nevirapene to prevent the transmission of HIV from mother to child, including the question of our countries being able to sustain such an intervention over the long term taking into account the cost of drugs.

• With regard to addressing the issue of the unaffordability of many drugs needed to treat our people even for sexually transmitted diseases and opportunistic infections, South Africa has passed a law allowing it to import cheaper drugs. Unfortunately, the pharmaceutical industry has decided to put profit before the people. The industry decided to sue the government on the basis that the law may interfere with their intellectual property rights. [The suit has been dropped.]

• Our health ministries have undertaken to strengthen the health services infra-structure to support persons with HIV/AIDS. Already our hospital beds are mainly occupied by patients with illnesses associated with AIDS who cannot be taken care of in the community.

• SADC is participating with the International Labour Organization to implement a Code of Conduct in the workplace to protect the rights of workers with HIV/AIDS. This will be in support of legislation that some countries have already passed to outlaw discrimination in the workplace.

There are many other examples I can cite to confirm that we in Africa take the HIV/AIDS epidemic seriously and are stepping up to the challenge but we cannot deny that as developing countries, our resources are limited. We therefore welcome the various forms of assistance that better resourced governments and organizations can provide . . .

On the legislative side we see many well-intentioned politicians taking the AIDS in Africa matter more seriously, resulting in many different bills. It would be a good idea to coordinate all these efforts so that we can have a few good bills with the potential of having a bigger impact.

Our appeal to our American friends is to ask you to join us as African Ambassadors and keep the matter of HIV/AIDS in your agenda, both here in the U.S. and abroad. Always keep this in mind, failure to contain this epidemic in Africa will not only be a disaster for the continent, but will inevitably affect the whole of humanity.

Someone recently said that the abbreviation A-I-D-S could also stand for AM I DOING SOMETHING? None of us should be caught napping. The world is counting on each and everyone of us to play a part in reversing the AIDS epidemic.

May I conclude by saying we are not in denial anymore. African leadership is committed and we are doing something about it.

7

The Chinese Government Is Hampering the Fight Against the AIDS Epidemic

Philip P. Pan

Philip P. Pan is a foreign correspondent in China for The Washington Post.

The Chinese government's position is that AIDS is a problem to be handled only by the government. As a result, individuals with AIDS who are desperate to get help, and grass-roots organizations that may want to address the AIDS issue are discouraged from speaking out about the disease. Generally, the Chinese government does not allow people with AIDS to be seen on television or to be interviewed by the media because if reporters were allowed to interview those with AIDS, the Chinese government's response to AIDS, which took several years, might be criticized. Furthermore, the public might complain about the poor condition of the Chinese health care system and about the government's role in collecting blood using unsafe procedures that possibly led to the infection of hundreds of thousands of Chinese peasants with AIDS. Experts warn that AIDS will spread quickly in China, where only a small fraction of the population knows about AIDS and where the government is acting too slowly and oppressively.

B etween sips of Coke at a McDonald's restaurant across from one of China's few AIDS clinics, a farmer from Henan province pleaded for help. Zhao Yong and his 9-year-old son are infected with HIV, the virus that causes AIDS. His wife died of the disease.

"I want to tell my story," said Zhao, 39, who sneaked out of the clinic because doctors barred reporters from visiting him there. "I want to appeal to society to save my life and my son's life. . . . We are desperate, and I am not afraid to speak out openly."

For the Chinese government, that's the problem. Three months after admitting it faces an AIDS epidemic, China convened its first national conference on AIDS and filmed a celebrity-studded television special to support AIDS sufferers. These were breakthroughs for a government that for years has all but ignored the disease. But something was missing from both events—people with HIV or AIDS. Only a few were allowed to appear.

Their absence highlights the political nature of the AIDS problem in China: The governing Communist Party wants to educate the public about a rapidly spreading disease, but is afraid of what might happen if people with HIV are permitted to speak freely and criticize the government.

"The government wants to stay in control of the message," said Wan Yanhai, a former Health Ministry official and AIDS activist who was not invited to the conference. "Their position is, AIDS is a problem for the government and the experts to solve, not for regular people and not for grass-roots organizations."

In that sense, the AIDS issue has thrown light once again on the troubles of an emerging civil society in China, where individuals and groups are striving to deal with problems openly but often find there are limits to what they can achieve in a political system that remains rigidly authoritarian.

About 600,000 people in China have been infected with HIV, according to the official estimate. A state-run newspaper reported last week [mid-November 2001] the actual figure could be five to 10 times higher.

If Chinese reporters were allowed to interview these people, the public would hear a flood of complaints—about Beijing's slow response to AIDS, about the health care system's inability to help those with the disease, and about the state's role in blood collections that may have infected hundreds of thousands of people.

Only a fraction of the Chinese public understands AIDS or cares much about those with the disease, and this works to the government's advantage politically. But health experts warn that a general lack of knowledge about AIDS, including basic facts about how it is transmitted, helps the disease spread more quickly. Widespread discrimination discourages many people from getting tested for HIV.

The AIDS issue has thrown light once again on the troubles of an emerging civil society in China.

"China needs a Ryan White," said one Chinese health official, referring to the American boy who helped shift U.S. public opinion about the disease in the 1980s. "But the government is afraid of what China's Ryan White might say."

Almost everyone with HIV or AIDS who appears on Chinese television has his or her face and voice obscured electronically. Those who appear in newspaper photographs usually have a thick black stripe covering their eyes. Many Chinese officials and journalists say this is done to protect people with HIV from further discrimination.

"Ideally, people with HIV would be able to stand up and face the camera without fear," said Fu Yan, a senior nurse at the AIDS clinic at Beijing's Youan Hospital. "But the pressure from society is too much. These people would lose their jobs and would be ostracized. So they don't want their faces shown."

AIDS patients want to be seen

But others who attended the AIDS conference argued that it would be easy for the government to find AIDS patients willing to be identified on television.

"By always disguising people with HIV, the media is sending the message that these people are different, and that AIDS is something shameful," said Ou Zhiyong, a health official from the western city of Chengdu. "There are definitely people willing to be identified. Many people with HIV are poor and can't afford treatment, and they want to go to the media and ask for help."

Only a fraction of the Chinese public understands AIDS or cares much about those with the disease, and this works to the government's advantage politically.

One person who has shown his face on television is Song Pengfei, a soft-spoken 19-year-old who was infected with HIV through a blood transfusion in 1998. The Chinese media embraced Song at first. But when he raised questions about China's blood supply at an international conference, the state-run media started ignoring him.

Only one HIV-positive person, 26-year-old AIDS educator Li Zhiyong, was permitted to speak at length at the conference, and only to a small gathering. Another patient, who remained anonymous, delivered brief remarks at the opening ceremony. Standing on a corner of a darkened stage, he thanked the Communist Party and the government for "giving me the courage to survive."

Taboo AIDS topics addressed

In other ways, though, the conference was groundbreaking. Several sessions broached topics that have long been taboo in China.

One panel discussed China's gay population, reporting that 10 percent to 15 percent of Chinese men have sex with other men, that most are married, and that many have multiple sexual partners and do not use condoms.

Rong Weiyi, a professor at a university run by the Public Security Ministry, even argued for gay rights and criticized police sweeps of gay bars, saying that such tactics force gays underground and make it more difficult to educate them about AIDS.

Another frank discussion occurred during a session on discrimination against people with HIV. Several health officials acknowledged that doctors and nurses often ask patients if they are HIV-positive and make them leave their hospitals if they are. Participants even debated whether people infected through blood transfusions are "more innocent" than those infected through drug use or sex.

For the most part, though, the subject of AIDS transmission through blood was off-limits during the meeting. Conference organizers required special approval for any paper on the subject.

The issue is a sensitive one because tens if not hundreds of thousands of impoverished peasants—including Zhao, the farmer from Henan province in central China—were infected with HIV after selling their blood to companies that used unsafe procedures and that were often run by local officials. No papers on the problem were presented at the conference.

Several speakers at the conference, including Health Minister Zhang Wenkang, emphasized the media's role in educating the public about AIDS. But only a handful of journalists were allowed to attend conference sessions.

Instead, the government apparently intends to reach the public through a carefully choreographed television special during prime time on Dec. 1, 2001, World AIDS Day.

The program will highlight the story of Li Ziliang, a peasant with HIV who struggled against discrimination. People refused to touch anything he touched, and his wife fled their home. But with the help of party and government officials, he found his wife and she returned to the family. A narrator tells the story, then Li himself appears on stage with his wife at his side to thunderous applause.

Li wears large, dark sunglasses and a baseball cap on stage, but Zou Youkai, the show's director, maintained that he "broke through the opaque glass that has been blocking out people with HIV."

"I knew from the start that I wanted someone with HIV to be on the stage, without any electronic distortion," Zou said. "This is a first for China."

But Zou said reporters would not be allowed to interview Li. "I think that would be too much pressure on him," he said. "I decided it would be best for him to just go home."

8

A Deadly Passage to India

Geoffrey Cowley

Geoffrey Cowley is a senior editor of Newsweek *and works as the magazine's health-and-medicine editor. Cowley has produced groundbreaking
stories on AIDS and other health issues, and his articles, including his
1990 piece entitled "AIDS: The Next Ten Years," have won numerous
awards as well as prompted government action.*

By the year 2010, India will have twenty to twenty-five million
people infected with AIDS. In spite of Indian government officials'
beliefs that their nation's moral character and conservative sexual
mores would keep AIDS from spreading there, poverty, illiteracy,
and a huge commercial sex trade have contributed alarmingly to
the spread of the disease. Part of India's commercial sex trade is
linked with their well-developed trucking transportation system.
Mothers trade sex at roadside truck-stops to feed their children
and truckdrivers spread the virus along their routes and then bring
it home to their wives. As a result of the spread of AIDS, the Indian political landscape has changed; Indian AIDS control agencies have won worldwide acclaim for their work with high-risk
groups, including sex workers and street children. However, these
are small victories in a country of one billion people. Hopefully,
with strong continued anti-AIDS efforts, the AIDS disease in India
will not reach epidemic proportions.

Wonder, degradation, hope—it's all on parade on a torrid summer
night in Kolkata's Kalighat district. Pilgrims are swarming in the
jasmine-scented mist outside the Dakshineswar Kali Temple. They've
come from all over India to pay homage to Kali, the fearsome Hindu god-
dess who continually devours whatever life the earth generates. The lane
leading up to the temple is a joyful riot of rickshaws, mopeds, stray goats
and street vendors. Inside, the mood approaches ecstasy as worshipers
burn incense and lay garlands and balloons at the feet of Kali's statue. But
the scene grows darker, and death more mundane, as you wander the
torch-lit lanes that extend behind the temple to the bank of the Hugli
River. Pigs forage freely at the waterfront for garbage and funeral-pyre
leftovers (open fires make imperfect incinerators). Men lounge on cots in

front of small huts while, inside, their wives perform sex acts on strangers for a few rupees. Kids play on the pavement amid pimps and johns who hunger to put them to work. The AIDS virus thrives in places like Kalighat, and Asia has many of them. That's one reason the region is now in such peril.

As the vanguard of what the CIA has dubbed the "next wave" of the global AIDS crisis, India and China could have 40 million HIV-positive people by the end of this decade—the same number the entire world has today. The CIA predicts that India alone will have 20 million to 25 million infections, up from 4 million today, "even if the disease does not break out significantly into the mainstream population." That's not to say that disaster is inevitable. Despite its widespread poverty, India has a growing economy and the rudiments of a health-care system. It also enjoys substantial support from international donors such as USAID and the Bill and Melinda Gates Foundation, which last week announced a new $100 million India initiative. But it will take more than money to stop this juggernaut. The challenge, says Dr. Helene Gayle of the Gates Foundation, is to create a national network of AIDS prevention programs to reach all those in need. As anyone traversing this vast country soon learns, that is a tall order.

Women have little say

AIDS has varied faces in a country this vast, but those of the women stand out. As I discovered in the Tamil town of Namakkal, a monogamous woman can earn her in-laws' contempt by getting infected by her husband. With their bright saris, almond eyes and shiny black hair, Chitra, Selvi, Suganda, Selvamani and Vanilla look more like college girls than widows. When the girls were in their late teens or early 20s, all five married truckdrivers and, in keeping with tradition, stayed home to care for babies or in-laws while their husbands plied the highways. All five are now HIV-positive, and all but one have nursed their mates through their own illness and death. The women still wear their wedding necklaces, still care for their young children. Yet each is now reviled by her in-laws. "The family always blames the wife," Suganda explains matter-of-factly. "Very few husbands will admit their own responsibility."

Kids play on the pavement amid pimps and johns who hunger to put them to work.

It's easy to feel for Suganda, harder to sympathize with whatever truck-stop prostitute propelled the virus into her life. Then you meet her, or someone like her, and realize what a small role that choice has played in her life. Pattamal is one of 500 young women working the trucks that stop for gas or repairs on a 30-mile stretch of road outside Chennai. She is not a derelict, not a party girl; she's a mom. Seated on a stool in the roadside office of a service organization called Santoshi, she strokes the hair of her quiet 6-year-old daughter and explains her strategy for keeping the child fed. When a driver propositions her on the roadside, she secures a commitment of 100 rupees ($2), then gives him 10 minutes behind a bush or in the cab of his truck. If the driver pays up, she makes as much as she would from a day of scrubbing floors, and hardly has to leave her daughter's side.

A disaster waiting to happen

How did India get into this mess? In many ways the country has been an AIDS disaster waiting to happen. Poverty and illiteracy are rife, and the commercial sex trade is huge. Women have little if any say in their sexual and reproductive lives. And a well-developed transportation system ensures that a sexually transmitted virus will spread widely once it arrives. When HIV arrived, in 1986, it had been battering other countries for five years, and its dynamics were well known. But instead of mobilizing to contain the virus, public officials blithely asserted that India's "moral character" and conservative sexual mores would keep it from spreading. The virus quickly defied that prediction, racing through red-light districts, infecting both sex workers and their clients. So the police started rounding up sex workers for mandatory blood tests, sometimes jailing the infected instead of promoting safer sex. Hospitals took a similar tack, using blood tests to expose and evict infected patients.

In many ways the country has been an AIDS disaster waiting to happen.

The political landscape is more hospitable today. The leaders of both major parties now acknowledge the urgency of the threat, and the country's AIDS-control agencies have won worldwide acclaim for their work with high-risk groups such as sex workers and street kids. Unfortunately, many average Indians are still living with more risk, and less protection, than they realize. Some 7 percent of the nation's adults harbor sexually transmitted infections—and nearly four men in 10 recall at least one homosexual encounter, according to surveys conducted by the Delhi-based Naz Foundation Trust. Sexuality was once a major theme in the culture. Tamil Nadu's temple sculptures offer elaborate taxonomies of sensual pleasure, both for couples and for trios ("One lady, two gents," as my guide politely observes). But the Kama Sutra spirit is not much in evidence today. Sex is largely absent from the Bollywood cinema, the mass media and casual conversation. Schools offer little or no sex education. And homosexuality is not only a moral offense but a legal one under Section 377 of the Indian Penal Code. If sex has become a difficult topic for ordinary Indians, AIDS is often an impossible one. Groups providing care for patients or orphans risk eviction if their landlords or neighbors discover their true mission. In several recent instances, local cops have detained of harassed outreach workers for distributing the government's own safe-sex education materials.

Where, then, is the basis for hope? A mom with other options would not turn $2 tricks on a roadside. A wife with other options would think twice about waiting on her in-laws while sex workers waited on her spouse. And children with options would surely look beyond the alleys of Kalighat for their livelihoods. No one—not even Bill Gates—can create such choices by fiat. But at every level of Indian society, one sees hints that change is possible. Pattamal may live humbly, but she learned about HIV in time to avoid contracting it herself. She has used condoms consistently for the past five years. As an educator for Santoshi, she now distributes them to her clients and her peers. In a benevolent pyramid scheme, she then enlists them to do the same. Similar programs have sprouted in most of India's red-light districts in recent years, and some have shown dramatic results.

A grass-roots sex workers' collective

In Kolkata's Sonagachi district, a grass-roots sex workers' collective called the Durbar Mahila Samanwaya Committee (DMSC) has held its 30,000 members' HIV rate below 10 percent for the past decade, even as the rates among other cities' sex workers has topped 50 percent. When members talk about the years before DMSC started in 1992, it's as though they're recalling bad dreams. Manju Biswas is typical. She was barely 13 when a neighbor in her village brought her to Kolkata on the pretext of finding her a job and sold her for $30 to a brothel keeper. Manju's father, a subsistence farmer, had died and her mother and brother were facing starvation. She was completely illiterate. "I was kept in a small, dark room locked for days by the madam," she told me. "Then one night I was forced to drink something that made me dizzy, and then this huge, drunken man was on top of me. I was screaming in pain but I fainted. When I woke up I was bleeding heavily. The madam told me I was now a fallen woman and should stop pestering her to let me go home. These men, 10 to 15 a day, would call on me. It was a horrible life."

If sex has become a difficult topic for ordinary Indians, AIDS is often an impossible one.

Through simple coalition-building, the DMSC gradually transformed the surrounding district and became a legitimate power broker. "We have now branches in almost all the towns and cities in West Bengal," says Swapna Gayen, DMSC's president. "We now sit across from officials and discuss matters relating to our health and welfare." The group also runs a 24-hour AIDS hot line that offers free medical and legal guidance to anyone seeking help.

Keeping their children out of the trade

Whatever their circumstances, few sex workers would choose prostitution for their daughters. While standing up for their own rights, most also do whatever they can to see their own children liberated entirely from the trade. On that front, too, signs of progress are easy to find. On the edge of Mumbai's crumbling Kamathipura red-light district, a group called Apne Aap has created a safe place for school-age girls (they call themselves "Sparrows") to read, paint and socialize. Another group, Sanlaap, runs a similar operation in Kolkata's Kalighat. Because this district's prostitutes work in their huts, the kids are essentially homeless from dusk until midnight. But for the past few years they have spent their evenings in Sanlaap's two concrete shacks, getting the encouragement and electric lights a kid needs to become literate. As I sat down with a dozen of the teens who frequent the drop-in center, its impact was palpable. All but two are in school. Seven are planning for college. And any one of them, even the 10-year-olds, can tell you how to avoid contracting HIV. The Sanlaap kids have recently launched a campaign to raise AIDS awareness within the red-light district—and the older ones are now seeking a wider audience. "We want to be leaders," says Sushmita, a poised 18-year-old who has just completed her college-entrance exam. "We want to show people outside Kalighat that a youth group from this district can make a difference."

Small victories add up, but neither the Kalighat kids nor the Sonagachi sex workers will transform a nation of 28 states, 24 languages and a billion people. It's one thing to get a child through school, quite another to shatter a legacy of fear, ignorance and stigma. Fortunately, bigger players are now embracing that goal. The Gates Foundation has yet to work out the details of its new $100 million program, but its immediate goal is to target the country's huge mobile population—not only truckers but also soldiers, railway workers and oil workers. The foundation has the clout to foster alliances among employers in all those sectors, and the freedom to cross the public-private divide. One can only guess how all these efforts will play out. What's clear is that Asia's infant plague does not have to grow into a disaster.

9

U.S. Pharmaceutical Companies and the U.S. Government Have Blocked the Availability of AIDS Drugs in Developing Countries

Robert Weissman

Robert Weissman is editor of Multinational Monitor *magazine and codirector of Essential Action, a corporate accountability group. He also is coauthor of* Corporate Predators: The Hunt for Megaprofits and the Attack on Democracy.

The United States government and U.S. pharmaceutical companies have actively opposed efforts by developing countries to make life-saving AIDS drugs more affordable and available in their countries. The efforts of these developing countries involve compulsory licensing and parallel importing, two ways of making AIDS drugs more affordable. Compulsory licensing would allow an African pharmaceutical company to manufacture a brand-name AIDS drug originally developed by a U.S. firm under a generic name. Compulsory licensing can lower the price of medicines by seventy-five percent or more. Parallel importing allows a company or a government agency to purchase AIDS medicines from industrialized countries at the lowest prices and resell them at these prices in their own countries. Although both of these practices are legal, U.S. pharmaceutical companies object to them on the grounds that they diminish corporate profits. The United States government has supported these pharmaceutical companies by withholding trade benefits from and threatening trade sanctions against developing countries for attempting to utilize compulsory licensing and parallel importing.

Robert Weissman, "AIDS and Developing Countries: Democratizing Access to Essential Medicines," *Foreign Policy in Focus*, vol. 4, August 31, 1999, p. 1. Copyright © 1999 by Interhemispheric Resource Center. Reproduced by permission.

O ne in eight South Africans, one in seven Kenyans, and one in four Zimbabweans has HIV/AIDS. U.S. Surgeon General David Satcher has likened the HIV/AIDS epidemic in Africa to the plague that decimated Europe in the fourteenth century.

Existing treatments, which enable many people with HIV/AIDS in the U.S. and other industrialized countries to live relatively healthy lives, are unavailable to all but a few people in Africa. Life-saving HIV/AIDS drug cocktails cost about $12,000 a year in many African countries—vastly out of reach of all but a small handful of the growing African population with HIV/AIDS.

Addressing the HIV/AIDS crisis in Africa and around the world will require a massively accelerated prevention effort. It will also require revitalizing the decimated public health systems of developing countries and making quality health care much more widely available. This, in turn, will require major new investments in public health and the abandonment of structural adjustment requirements to collect "user fees" from people seeking health care. But for millions of people infected with the HIV virus, there is also a crying need to make life-saving drugs more available—and quickly.

Compulsory licensing and parallel imports

Two ways to promote access to essential medicines involve compulsory licensing and parallel imports. The more important of these policy tools, compulsory licensing, enables any government to instruct a patent holder to license the right to use its patent to a company, government agency, or other party. Zimbabwe, for example, could issue a license to a local company for an HIV/AIDS drug manufactured by Bristol-Myers Squibb. The Zimbabwean firm would then manufacture the drug for sale in Zimbabwe under a generic name, and it would pay a reasonable royalty to Bristol-Myers Squibb on each sale.

Compulsory licensing lowers prices to consumers by creating competition in the market for the patented good. Its impact is similar to the introduction of generic competition at the end of a drug's patent term—prices come tumbling down. Compulsory licensing can lower the price of medicines by 75% or more.

Parallel imports involve imports of a product from one country and resale, without authorization of the original seller, in another, thereby allowing the buyer to search for the lowest world price. A Namibian company or government agency, for example, might purchase HIV/AIDS drugs in France—assuming they are sold for a lower price in France—and then resell them in Namibia. Since the price of medicines is sometimes lower in the United States and other industrialized countries, parallel imports can be a tool to enable developing countries to lower prices for consumers.

Both compulsory licensing and parallel imports are permitted under the international trade rules established by the General Agreement on Tariffs and Trade (GATT) and administered by the World Trade Organization (WTO). They are regularly used in industrialized countries, including the United States, Japan, and the European Union. One of the GATT agreements, the Agreement on Trade-Related Aspects of Intellectual Property Rights (TRIPS), contains the international rules the WTO enforces on intellectual property (patents, copyrights, and trademarks). Industry, especially the pharmaceutical sector, exercised heavy influence over the TRIPS agreement negotiations, and many public interest advocates generally believe the TRIPS agreement inappropriately favors corporations.

Existing treatments, which enable many people with HIV/AIDS in the U.S. . . . to live relatively healthy lives, are unavailable to all but a few people in Africa.

In general, the TRIPS agreement requires countries to adopt U.S.-style patent systems, which apply both to products and processes and last for 20 years. This has compelled many developing countries—which had followed the lead of virtually every industrialized country in enacting weak patent rules while they were still industrializing (many European countries did not recognize patents until the 1970s)—to refashion their patent rules dramatically.

But whatever the TRIPS agreement's biases, and despite the requirements it imposes on signatory countries, it permits compulsory licensing and parallel imports. Yet, despite the WTO-legality of these policy tools, multinational pharmaceutical companies object to the practices, which they perceive as curtailing corporate profits. The U.S. government has adopted a similar view, strongly opposing developing country efforts to undertake compulsory licensing, parallel imports, or other similar measures to make HIV/AIDS drugs and other essential medicines more available and affordable to their people.

Some key points

• Africa and the developing world are facing an HIV/AIDS crisis equated by the U.S. surgeon general to the plague that decimated Europe in the fourteenth century.

• Combination of available pharmaceuticals—too expensive for nearly all of the infected people in the developing world—could enable many afflicted with HIV/AIDS to live relatively normal lives.

• Compulsory licensing and parallel importing policies could help developing country governments make essential medicines more affordable to their citizens.

Despite the legality of compulsory licensing and parallel imports, and despite the public health emergency enveloping much of the developing world, the U.S. has actively opposed developing country efforts to implement compulsory licensing, parallel imports, or other measures to make life-saving HIV/AIDS drugs more affordable and available in their countries. Although it frequently argues—incorrectly—that compulsory licensing and the other measures are WTO-illegal, the U.S. also takes the position that it has the right and authority to demand that countries do even more to protect intellectual property rights than is required by the TRIPS agreement.

To justify this position, Washington echoes pharmaceutical industry claims that compulsory licensing unfairly impinges on corporate intellectual property rights. The companies' unstated, overarching concern is that the United States and other industrialized nations might follow developing countries in pursuing compulsory licensing and parallel imports to lower consumer prices. These industry claims, however, ignore the fact that compulsory licensing is part of the intellectual property system—it is one of the many limitations on patent rights, and patent holders know this when they receive a patent. In the United States, for example, compulsory licenses are regularly issued on products ranging from pesticides to pollution control devices to computer processing chips. And under WTO compulsory licensing rules, companies receive reasonable royalties when a patented invention is used.

Questions about research and development

The U.S. also champions the pharmaceutical industry's argument that the high cost of research and development (R&D) requires that companies be given freedom to charge whatever they want. But it is unreasonable to give a blank check to anyone who controls life-saving technologies. And several facts cast doubt on industry claims about R&D and profits, especially in the case of the developing world.

First, governments often finance the key R&D costs of important drugs. In the case of HIV/AIDS, for example, the two leading candidates for compulsory licensing are AZT and ddI, both of which were developed at the National Institutes of Health (NIH) at U.S. taxpayer expense. Both drugs have already generated huge profits for drug companies. Second, the drug companies routinely exaggerate the costs of developing new drugs.

There is a moral issue: should people with HIV/AIDS in poor countries be denied available treatments so that companies can earn higher profits?

Third, since compulsory licensing will increase company sales (as it lowers prices), this policy tool may not harm industry earnings at all, or it may hurt earnings less than initially appears to be the case. If compulsory licensing expands access to AZT and ddI in Africa and the developing world without undermining high prices in the U.S. and Europe, the companies could come out ahead, since they are currently selling so little in developing country markets.

Fourth, developing country markets are a paltry income source for the multinational drug companies—representing only about 10% of international sales, 1.6% in the case of Africa. Lower revenues from developing countries, should they occur, would not affect company R&D efforts or profitability to any significant extent. Application of the intellectual property system in developing countries won't make much of a dent in company profits one way or another, but it can make a huge difference in people's access to medicines.

Finally, there is a moral issue: should people with HIV/AIDS in poor countries be denied available treatments so that companies can earn higher

profits? Neither compulsory licensing nor parallel imports involves companies selling their products at a loss.

These are not just academic arguments. The U.S. has exerted extraor-
dinary pressure on developing countries to prevent them from pursuing
compulsory licensing and similar strategies to make drugs widely available. Most notably, Washington has undertaken a massive bullying effort
to get South Africa to repeal provisions of its Medicines Act that would
help the country make essential medicines more accessible and affordable.

A report from the State Department says, "All relevant agencies of the
U.S. government—the Department of State together with the Department
of Commerce, its U.S. Patent and Trademark Office, the Office of the
United States Trade Representative, the National Security Council and the
Office of the Vice President—have been engaged in an assiduous, concerted campaign to persuade the government of South Africa to withdraw
or modify" the Medicines Act provisions that give the government the
authority to pursue compulsory licensing and parallel import policies.
The State Department report explains how "U.S. government agencies
have been engaged in a full court press with South African officials from
the departments of Trade and Industry, Foreign Affairs, and Health" to
pressure them to change the law. [Former] Vice President Al Gore has
raised the issue repeatedly with South Africa's former Deputy President
(now President) Thabo Mbeki.

The United States has withheld certain trade benefits from South
Africa and has threatened trade sanctions (by putting South Africa on the
"Special 301 Watch List" of countries receiving heightened U.S. scrutiny
regarding trading practices) as punishment for Pretoria's refusal to repeal
those provisions of its Medicines Act that offend the multinational drug
companies. Washington has also enlisted the French, Swiss, and German
presidents to raise the issue with top South African officials.

And South Africa is not alone. Washington has undertaken similar actions against other countries—chiefly, Argentina, Brazil, Thailand, and
India—that have enacted or considered intellectual property rules that
would make essential medicines more affordable to their citizens.

Some key problems

• Without access to existing HIV/AIDS treatments, millions of people in
developing countries are sentenced to preventable deaths.

• Washington is pressuring developing countries not to adopt compulsory licensing and other intellectual property policies that could make
HIV/AIDS drugs more affordable.

• U.S. government positions on intellectual property questions are re-
sponsive to corporate greed, not public health needs.

Toward a new foreign policy

In May 1999, the World Health Assembly, the policymaking body of the
World Health Organization (WHO), passed a resolution that declared public health concerns "paramount" in intellectual property issues related to
pharmaceuticals. Although Washington had vociferously opposed earlier
efforts to obtain passage of a similar resolution that said public health con-

cerns should take priority over commercial matters, the U.S., after insist-ing on minor changes, voted in support of the 1999 resolution. It is now time for Washington to bring its foreign policy into compliance with the accepted notion that public health protection is the most important goal in shaping pharmaceutical patent policy.

First, the U.S. should announce that it will terminate all bilateral pres-sure on South Africa, Thailand, Brazil, Argentina, India, and other coun-tries for pursuing compulsory licensing policies, parallel imports, or any other WTO-legal policy. Instead, Washington should formally declare that it accepts the legitimacy of compulsory licensing and should imme-diately lift all sanctions currently in place against countries in retaliation for pursuing any intellectual property policies designed to make vital medicines more available to those in need.

Second, pending legislation should be altered. The African Growth and Opportunity Act currently conditions new benefits to developing countries on whether they enforce "appropriate policies relating to pro-tection of intellectual property rights." Such provisions should either not be enacted into law or should be revised to clarify that "appropriate poli-cies" include compulsory licensing and other measures that help to make life-saving drugs more widely available.

Third, rather than using the millennial round of WTO negotiations in Seattle [in the] fall [of 1999] to tighten intellectual property require-ments related to pharmaceuticals, the U.S. should lead the way in calling for a review of the existing TRIPS agreement and its effect on access to HIV/AIDS and other essential medicines. Among the pertinent questions: Have TRIPS rules undermined the ability of developing countries to main-tain domestic pharmaceutical industries? If so, what impact has this had on consumers? Have TRIPS rules promoted new multinational corporate investment in research to treat and prevent diseases of particular concern to developing countries?

Fourth, the U.S. should immediately license to the WHO all of the HIV/AIDS drugs that have been developed with government funding and for which the U.S. government holds patent or other intellectual property rights. Existing law permits Washington to take such steps. With a li-cense, the WHO could contract with private generic makers to produce the medicines and distribute them widely in the developing world. Since many of the most important HIV/AIDS remedies—such as ddI—were de-veloped with significant U.S. government funding, the U.S. government controls rights to many important HIV/AIDS treatment pharmaceuticals.

Finally, it should be reiterated that although access to essential med-icines is of critical importance, much more must also be done to prevent the spread of HIV/AIDS and to improve treatment of those infected. An essential step in combating the transmission of this disease is to cancel the foreign debts of the poorest countries, since debt servicing siphons off funds from investment in public health. World Bank and IMF structural adjustment programs that impose policies—such as requiring copay-ments from indigent patients—also make it more difficult for those with HIV/AIDS to gain access to medical care. And African governments must do more to support AIDS education and prevention efforts and to destig-matize people with the disease.

10

U.S. Pharmaceutical Companies Have Helped Make AIDS Drugs Available in Developing Countries

John Siegfried

John Siegfried is a doctor who serves as a senior medical officer for the Pharmaceutical Research and Manufacturers of America (PhRMA), a trade association representing the American research-based pharmaceutical industry. Siegfried has worked as a volunteer physician caring for AIDS patients at the Elizabeth Taylor Medical Center, a leading AIDS facility in Washington, D.C.

The United States pharmaceutical industry has led the way in producing anti-HIV/AIDS medicines to help those suffering with AIDS around the world. In only a decade and a half, the industry has developed fifty-four AIDS medicines and has plans to develop over one hundred more, including an HIV vaccine. Bristol-Myers Squibb is spending $100 million over five years to fund AIDS research trials in five African Countries and to help organizations bolster community AIDS prevention and treatment programs. Bristol-Myers Squibb is also donating drugs to Mexico to treat pediatric AIDS. Another pharmaceutical company, GlaxoSmithKline, is providing sharply reduced prices for AZT, a drug used to combat mother-to-child AIDS transmission. Glaxo Wellcome is also sponsoring a program in developing countries called Positive Action, which provides intensive training to community groups and nongovernment organizations (NGO's) for delivering improved HIV/AIDS care.

In the area of therapies for HIV/AIDS, the contribution made by the U.S. pharmaceutical industry is nothing short of remarkable. The first reports of a mysterious illness, later identified as HIV/AIDS, appeared in the medical literature in 1981 and the HIV virus was identified in 1983. The

John Siegfried, testimony on behalf of the Pharmaceutical Research and Manufacturers of America before the House Government Reform Committee, July 22, 1999.

44

first HIV/AIDS treatment was approved only in 1987. Since then 54 medicines have been approved for HIV/AIDS and associated conditions, and an additional 113 are in development, most of which are being developed by the research-intensive pharmaceutical companies. Government and academic scientists generally led the way in advancing basic knowledge about HIV/AIDS, although pharmaceutical companies have contributed. And the industry has led the way in translating those advances in knowledge into anti-HIV/AIDS medicines to help patients.

Pharmaceutical companies led the discovery and development of medicines to help HIV/AIDS patients.

Drug discovery and development in the U.S. usually takes 12 to 15 years from the test tube to the pharmacy. The development of 54 medicines within only a decade and a half is thus an unprecedented accomplishment. The National Institutes of Health, particularly the National Institute of Allergy and Infectious Disease with its Division of AIDS, led in advancing our basic knowledge. Pharmaceutical companies led the discovery and development of medicines to help HIV/AIDS patients. And the Food and Drug Administration expedited review and approval of these life-saving medicines.

Equally unprecedented are the results of this effort in the United States, and in many other developed countries. The death rate from AIDS in the U.S. dropped by nearly one-half from 1997 to 1998—the largest single year decline in any major cause of death ever. The health of many HIV-positive patients improved. Many have returned, and are returning, to work and leading more productive lives. Often the demand for more expensive secondary and tertiary health care services has declined as a result of newer therapies, providing the most cost-effective health care for HIV/AIDS patients. The new products not only best help many patients, but also can reduce the need for other medicines to treat the diseases associated with AIDS and the need for treatments in hospitals and hospices.

The foundation on which this progress rests is investment in innovative research and development. And it is in the area of applied research and development that the pharmaceutical industry excels. It is the industry's role in this crisis to lead the way in the discovery and development of pharmaceutical and biotechnology products that can play a critical role in HIV/AIDS treatment and prevention. But not all patients and not all countries can afford them. Effective responses to the HIV/AIDS challenge in developing nations must take into consideration all the relevant factors, including medical infrastructure, available resources, disease awareness and prevention initiatives and, most importantly, national commitment and leadership to make HIV/AIDS a public health priority.

The role of the research-based
U.S. pharmaceutical industry

The principal role of the research-based U.S. pharmaceutical industry in confronting HIV/AIDS world-wide is to continue what it does best—to marshal the expertise and capacity in applied biomedical research and drug development to discover new and more effective treatments. In co-operation and collaboration with scientists in the government and academia, some pharmaceutical companies are also seeking to discover and develop an effective HIV vaccine, which ultimately would be the most effective and cost-effective way to prevent HIV/AIDS and to respond to the global AIDS pandemic.

Investors in pharmaceutical companies seek a return on their investment commensurate with the large risk they assume. The current cost of bringing a pharmaceutical product to market averages $500 million, and only one of five to ten thousand compounds tested ever reaches the marketplace. Additionally, of marketed products, on average only one in three generates revenues that meet or exceed average Research and Development (R&D) costs. The U.S. pharmaceutical industry is spending $24 billion on research and development, including [in 1999] approximately $2 billion on research and development of HIV/AIDS-related drugs. Over 20 percent of all domestic sales revenues go back into research and development—the highest proportion of any industry with which we are familiar. Intellectual property protection and market pricing are the keystones of, and are essential to, this research effort.

Many countries lack the broad public health infrastructure necessary to support the use of complex regimens of anti-HIV treatments.

The research-based U.S. pharmaceutical industry has contacts with government and health agencies around the world and, therefore, is well positioned to provide input in the area of national health education and policy. This expertise complements and supplements the responsibilities and expertise of other members of the world health care community, both public and private.

Let me give you several examples:

• Bristol-Myers Squibb is spending $100 million over five years in five southern African countries to fund extensive AIDS research trials, improve training for more than 200 physicians, and help non-governmental organizations bolster community AIDS-prevention and treatment programs. The company also has developed a pediatric AIDS program in Mexico, donating drugs to cover all untreated cases of pediatric AIDS in the country and providing physician training and community outreach.

• The Merck Company Foundation is underwriting the Enhancing Care Initiative, an initiative coordinated by the Harvard AIDS Institute and the Francois-Xavier Bagnoud Center for Health and Human Rights at the Harvard School of Public Health. The Enhancing Care Initiative will address the issue of HIV/AIDS in the developing world by bringing together the best possible expertise within specific countries, including representatives of the local HIV community. The goal is to customize specific, practical improvements that will help to advance the quality, delivery and outcomes of HIV care for men, women and children living with HIV/AIDS, not only in the initial countries selected (beginning with

Senegal and Brazil), but in a broad range of developing countries throughout the world.

• Glaxo Wellcome is providing deeply discounted prices for AZT, [azidothymidine] to combat mother-child vertical transmission, in cooperation with UNAIDS [United Nations joint program for AIDS]. In addition, the company is sponsoring a program called Positive Action. Positive Action's activities are devoted to initiatives and organizations in developing countries. For example, intensive training is provided to developing country community groups and non-government organizations that identify and meet local needs to improve the delivery of HIV/AIDS care. The company also founded the Global Business Council on HIV/AIDS, a consortium of private and public sector groups whose objectives are to advance private sector HIV workplace policies.

These activities in the private sector complement the initiatives of others—including the HIV community, governments, and international organizations.

Broadening access to modern health care in developing countries, including pharmaceuticals, is a complex challenge. While the HIV/AIDS pandemic creates special challenges, the needs of patients world-wide with tuberculosis, cancer, parasitic and fungal infections does not lag far behind. Many countries lack the broad public health infrastructure necessary to support the use of complex regimens of anti-HIV treatments. Many AIDS experts, such as Dr. Thomas Coates, Executive Director of the University of California at San Francisco's AIDS Research Institute, have been quoted as saying that delivery of complex, demanding AIDS drugs without the necessary infrastructure and supervision is a "recipe for disaster." It is neither feasible nor desirable to simply import treatment regimens from other countries into South Africa. This is true for the disease HIV/AIDS and for many other health conditions. These are complex issues that can only be addressed through collaborations involving industry, government, international organizations, patient and medical groups. All are vital to finding workable solutions that will help patients with HIV/AIDS lead better lives and prevent others from contracting AIDS.

11

Rich and Poor Nations Should Collaborate in the Development of an AIDS Vaccine

Malegapuru William Makgoba, Nandipha Solomon, and Timothy Johan Paul Tucker

Malegapuru William Makgoba is the president of the Medical Research Council of South Africa. Nandipha Solomon is the executive manager for corporate communications and marketing for the council. Timothy Johan Paul Tucker is the director of the South African AIDS Vaccine Initiative.

Despite the complex political and scientific challenges to the development of an AIDS vaccine, scientists expect to have an affordable and effective vaccine to combat this disease by the year 2010. Partnerships between researchers, manufacturers, and distributors, as well as partnerships between rich and poor countries, are essential for the successful development of a vaccine. In addition to these partnerships, it is important to establish rules for the distribution of new vaccines to assure that the poorest and highest at-risk populations receive them.

HIV infections and deaths from AIDS continue to ravage many countries around the world, with most infected people living in the poorest nations. In terms of morbidity and mortality, the HIV/AIDS pandemic is worse than the Black Death of the 14th century. The search for an HIV vaccine was seen as the logical solution to the burgeoning epidemic soon after the discovery of HIV, but early enthusiasm became muted as the realities of the challenge became evident.

Nevertheless, there are scientific reasons why there is hope that an HIV vaccine will ultimately be developed. Firstly, studies of non-human primates that were given candidate vaccines based on HIV or SIV (simian immunodeficiency virus) have shown either complete or partial protec-

Malegapuru William Makgoba, Nandipha Solomon, and Timothy Johan Paul Tucker, "The Search for an HIV Vaccine," *British Medical Journal*, vol. 324, January 26, 2002, p. 211. Copyright © 2002 by *British Medical Journal*. Reproduced by permission.

tion against infection with the wild type virus. Secondly, successful vaccines have been developed against other retroviruses. Thirdly, almost all humans develop some form of immune response to HIV infection, with some exposed people remaining uninfected or developing immune responses that are protective or that are able to control the viral infection over long periods. Some people have remained free of disease for up to 20 years, often with undetectable viral loads. A group of sex workers from Nairobi and South Africa has remained HIV negative despite continuing high risk exposure; resistance to HIV infection in these people is thought to be due to their ability to mount protective immune responses to HIV, rather than to any innate host genetic factors. This group has provided insights into strategies for developing a vaccine.

Will an appropriate HIV vaccine ever be developed?

The answer to this depends on a complex interplay of politics, science, institutions and their organisation, and public-private partnerships.

Political realities need to be accepted

Many political realities will need to be accepted if the global health community is to develop an HIV vaccine:

• Vaccines are a public good and should be supported worldwide.

• Rich countries have the expertise and experience to develop and test HIV vaccines but do not have sufficient numbers of patients to conduct clinical trials of efficacy.

• Most poor countries have poor infrastructure and inadequate resources to conduct major trials of an HIV vaccine but are fertile ground for such trials. Thus, rich and poor nations are obliged to cooperate in the successful development of an HIV vaccine.

• Any trial of an HIV vaccine must take into account the history of exploitation and abuse of vulnerable people in clinical trials. All research has the potential to introduce unequal power relations between the researchers and the trial participants, particularly when the researchers are from a rich nation and the participants are from a poor nation.

• Rich countries want to do research in poor countries. Poor countries often have weak research infrastructure and regulatory institutions, allowing rich countries to exert more control over the research and over intellectual property rights.

• Most countries lack the political will and commitment—reflected in inadequate investment—to develop an HIV vaccine.

Science still inadequate

The current impressive knowledge of the genotypic, phenotypic, pathological, and clinical aspects of HIV/AIDS reflects the substantial scientific discourse that has occurred around the world over the past two decades. However, the current knowledge base remains inadequate, in that it has failed to elucidate the most critical item on the HIV vaccinologist's wish list: the correlates of protection against HIV. Until these are defined with accuracy, as has been the case with other infectious agents, such as hepatitis B, the required "height of the high jump bar" will remain speculative.

Another problem is that animal models for investigating candidate vaccines are inadequate. Results from studies of candidate vaccines in small animal models are invaluable, but their applicability to the development of an HIV vaccine in humans may be tenuous. Products that have an acceptable safety record in animal studies should be used as rapidly as possible in human studies, because human studies will give critical insights into the potential success or failure of a vaccine that far outweigh those from any animal data.

A coordinated international effort

Science has traditionally moved relatively slowly and cautiously in the transition from laboratory development of new agents to commercialisation. Yet in the case of HIV vaccines the scientific community is, for humanitarian reasons, under pressure to move with urgency. The scientific and corporate communities are being asked to "think out of the box" and to break down traditional modes of operations, while still maintaining the highest values of science and ethics, in developing an HIV vaccine.

For almost a decade after the discovery of HIV a concerted and coordinated international effort to produce a vaccine was slow to develop. But a number of initiatives have helped to create a scientific framework for rapidly testing hypotheses and products. The International AIDS Vaccine Initiative (IAVI), whose mission is the development of and worldwide access to an HIV vaccine, has helped to keep the need for a vaccine high on the agendas of many governments. Following from IAVI's advocacy, changes in the scientific priorities of traditional institutions, such as the National Institutes of Health, the World Health Organization (WHO) and the European Union's HIV vaccine platform, have also helped, as has the establishment of regional vaccine development programmes in poor countries, such as the South African AIDS Vaccine Initiative.

Even when we do develop an HIV vaccine, there is no guarantee that it will be used appropriately.

This new framework gives the public and private sectors the chance to become partners in getting important academic, financial, and logistic support. Effective coordination, maintenance, and expansion of these structures are essential. Equally important is the need for cooperation among these international bodies, to ensure that the efforts are not inhibited by organisational pride, traditions, or the desire to be first.

Levels of political will to support global initiatives to develop an HIV vaccine will largely determine the rate of their progress and success. Such political support will need to come from the highest levels of government and from global bodies such as the United Nations. Vaccines are but a part of the message of prevention that all governments should be endorsing, along with progressive policies on sex education, condom distribution, needle exchange programmes, and appropriate treatment. State and private sector funding of national and international vaccine programmes should be given the highest priority.

Political support for these programmes needs to be independent of other international crises. For example, our response to the [September 11, 2001, terrorist attacks on America] should not deflect attention from the urgent need to develop a vaccine against the greatest threat ever to humanity from an infectious disease. Yet compare the rapid and committed response by the US government to the threat of anthrax with many governments' lack of support for development of an HIV vaccine over the past two decades.

Public-private partnerships

Political processes should seek to maximise the synergies between government and the private sector through public-private partnerships. Over decades the private sector has been the mainstay of vaccine production and distribution, and thus the private sector's expertise needs to be harnessed to produce and distribute an appropriate HIV vaccine.

Vaccines are the only hope for the control and possible elimination of HIV infection.

Vaccines have never been as commercially successful as other medical treatments, and so entering the field of HIV vaccine development is a risk for companies. Most of the initial uptake of an effective vaccine will have to be in countries with a high prevalence; and as these countries are heavily indebted, they will not have the resources to buy and distribute the vaccine. Governments of the rich countries will have to work with IAVI, the World Bank, the United Nations, the WHO, and the private sector to ensure that commercial guarantees are in place to give the private sector an incentive to move into this field. These commercial agreements will have to give attention to:
- Setting limits on exploitation of intellectual property,
- "Guaranteed" markets,
- Price controls in poor countries,
- Limiting liability in the event of a small number of adverse events (such as with polio), and
- Ways to increase global manufacturing capacity.

Equally important will be the need for all countries, irrespective of wealth, to develop strategies to incorporate HIV vaccines into national vaccination programmes.

What will we do with an HIV vaccine?

New rules for vaccine and drug distribution

Even when we do develop an HIV vaccine, there is no guarantee that it will be used appropriately. This is why we should determine the rules for access to and distribution of the vaccine before making it widely available. The rules for distribution of an HIV vaccine must break with the present rules for access to new drugs and vaccines whereby priority is given to wealthy nations and people, who do not bear the burden of this disease. We see this problem in the current unequal access to antiretroviral drugs. HIV vaccines must be given firstly to the poorest and most vulnerable people in our global society. This will be a difficult challenge, as our current experience with polio vaccines in poor countries has shown, where warfare and social dislocation have often prevented the distribution of vaccines.

High risk populations in rich countries will also need to be targeted. Commercial sex workers, high risk gay men, haemophiliac people, injecting drug users, and children born to HIV positive mothers will need to be protected (or partially protected) by these vaccines. To ensure adequate manufacture and distribution of the vaccine, we will need accurate measures of the numbers of people in different regions that will require vaccination. This will be a difficult task that will need to involve governments and society.

How the vaccine will be used initially will be determined by the rates of full and partial protection given by the early generation of vaccines. If the early vaccines offer only marginal protection, there may be reason to use these only in high risk groups and then wait for more successful vaccines to be developed for use in lower risk groups. The same principle applies to any major side effects: these will be tolerated by and be acceptable to low risk populations only in the setting of very high predicted levels of protection.

Timing of administration of HIV vaccines will be complex and will need to take local factors into consideration. Decisions will need to be made whether to include HIV vaccines from birth in an expanded immunisation programme or whether to wait until pre-adolescence (or whether to immunise at both ages). Data on protection in these two settings of vertical and sexual transmission will help in these decisions. . . .

It is generally agreed that the development of an affordable, appropriate, and effective HIV vaccine is within reach—within 7–10 years. Vaccines are the only hope for the control and possible elimination of HIV infection, as was the case with smallpox and polio, which have been fully or partially eliminated by global vaccination programmes. How we distribute the vaccine will be a test of our international ethics and humanitarian objectives, and our generation will be judged by its success or failure in making a vaccine and ensuring equitable access to it.

12

The Collaboration of Rich and Poor Nations in AIDS Research Creates Ethical Problems

Paul Farmer

Paul Farmer is a professor of social medicine at Harvard Medical School and a world-renowned social medical activist. Dr. Farmer, an advocate for the poor and the suffering of the developing world, works with the Partners for Health and as an adviser on infectious diseases to the governments of several nations. Dr. Farmer lives and works most of the year in a village in Haiti.

When wealthy nations perform medical research in poorer countries, including research for AIDS medicines, ethical problems arise. One problem is that there are no practical guidelines to assure that participants from developing countries who volunteer in the research studies understand the purpose of the studies or what it means when they sign a consent form to participate in the research. In addition, the social inequality between the rich researcher and the poor subject creates gaps in the outcomes of the research projects. These problems need to be analyzed and understood to create a climate for ethical AIDS research in developing countries.

R esearchers are increasingly aware of infectious diseases that mainly affect poor people. Some diseases, like AIDS, were unknown only a generation ago; others, including tuberculosis and malaria, are now resurgent in new and more difficult-to-treat forms. These three diseases will probably kill 6 million people [in 2002] alone, and social inequalities are central to the emergence of these pandemics. Identification of new methods of diagnosis, drugs, and control strategies is of the utmost importance if medical and public-health workers hope to control these diseases in the settings in which they take their greatest toll.

Paul Farmer, "Can Transnational Research Be Ethical in the Developing World?" *The Lancet,* October 26, 2002, p. 1,266. Copyright © 2002 by *The Lancet.* Reproduced by permission.

It is not surprising, then, that thousands of research projects link affluent universities in developed countries with slums and villages in the less-developed world. Nor is it surprising that these collaborations are beset with difficulties and controversies: the social context is one, after all, of deepening inequalities between rich and poor. The past decade has been marked by many debates, often buried deep in the columns of our professional journals, about the ethics of transnational research projects. Are institutional review boards, irrespective of their constitution, capable of monitoring research across such steep grades of inequality? Is truly ethical research possible in poor communities?

Disparities grow with social inequalities, and social inequalities are little understood by either medical ethicists or medical researchers.

Daniel Fitzgerald [a researcher from Cornell University Medical College] and colleagues, writing from Haiti, take up the debate from a starting point that few would dispute: "Unfortunately, there are few practical guidelines on how best to inform research volunteers or how to ensure their understanding of the consent form." The data they present stem in part from a questionnaire, a series of true or false questions relevant to HIV-1 transmission, the topic of the study for which volunteers were being recruited. Although detailed social characteristics of the cohort are not included, most participants were poor and illiterate city-dwellers; all were negative for HIV-1, and had had sexual contact with someone infected with HIV-1 (Gheskio, the site of the survey, is urban Haiti's largest source of free care for sexually transmitted infections and for some complications of HIV; the centre has offered many of these services for 20 years).[1]

Fitzgerald and colleagues found that only three of the 15 volunteers passed the test. They showed that counselling sessions with a non-physician psychologist could substantially increase the proportion of volunteers able to pass the qualifying exam. This small study suggests that modest investments in better communication can improve participants' understanding of the process in which they are being engaged.

If the goal of such an exercise is merely to increase the number of volunteers who can pass an exam, the debate might end there. But although improvement of tools such as those for informed consent is a fine goal, sights should not be set too low. Focusing on only the process can lead to an overemphasis on the consent form (or institutional review board) as the key to rendering research in such settings ethical.

The fact that so few volunteers could pass the simple test is a reminder that, increasingly, researcher and subject are living in two different worlds. Counselling sessions before signing a consent form do not change the social conditions that structure the growing gap, cognitive and social, between those who do research and those who are participants. These social gaps underpin the growing "outcome gap" that characterises transnational

---

1. HIV-1 and HIV-2 are the two major viruses that cause AIDS.

research projects. Empirical research on the process of informed consent across this gap is urgently needed.

Social inequalities create disparities

Fitzgerald and colleagues' study allows a frank discussion of what is at stake as inequalities of risk grow for certain diseases. Disparities grow with social inequalities, and social inequalities are little understood by either medical ethicists or medical researchers; thus, this and other sincere attempts to address social context are welcome.

Social context is not merely local, nor are standards of care. In studies linking developed and less-developed countries, context is transnational, and such research is a reminder that some populations are not really developing, but rather being left behind by the same global economic processes that enable powerful universities to do research in poor countries. Does this disparity mean that research should not be done at all in such settings? Such Luddite responses need to be anticipated and prepared for to defend research in less-developed countries if researchers can answer local demands for equity and criticisms of the uses to which findings are put. This process will be best helped by in-depth social analysis of inequalities between countries and plans to remedy them. In studies of AIDS, research might have to be linked to access to the best treatment available, rather than to local standards of care.

All medical and public-health researchers would like a magic bullet that would make research undeniably ethical. But there is no magic bullet. There is only the complex and difficult process of linking research in resource-poor settings to the services demanded by poor people. The alternative prospect—a world in which medical research is dedicated wholly to the diseases of the affluent—is too painful to contemplate.

13

The Development of an AIDS Vaccine Is Not a "Magic Bullet" Solution

Committee on HIV Prevention
Strategies in the United States

The Committee on HIV Prevention Strategies in the United States reports on a project funded by the Centers for Disease Control and Prevention and is part of the Division of Health Promotion and Disease Prevention of the Institute of Medicine.

The development of a universally effective AIDS vaccine is unlikely due to the high level of mutability and the different modes of transmission of HIV, the virus believed to cause AIDS, and the different biological characteristics of populations affected by the virus. In addition to these obstacles, fundamental scientific and economic barriers to the development of an AIDS vaccine include a dearth of adequate animal models on which to test the effectiveness of vaccines and a lack of knowledge about the immune response needed to prevent HIV. Economically, the development of an AIDS vaccine is commercially risky because it is expensive and time consuming and companies don't know if they will receive significant financial returns from their work on the vaccine.

The development of a protective vaccine for HIV infection has been a primary goal since the beginning of the HIV/AIDS epidemic. Research has focused on developing both a preventive vaccine, which would prevent infection or prevent development of symptoms in those infected but asymptomatic, and a therapeutic vaccine, which would slow or stop progression of disease in infected, symptomatic individuals.

Despite significant advances in understanding of the virus, its biology, and its interaction with the human body, fundamental scientific and economic barriers hinder the development of a human vaccine for HIV. First, there are no adequate animal models in which to test the efficacy of

Committee on HIV Prevention Strategies in the United States, *No Time to Lose: Getting More from HIV Prevention*, edited by Monica S. Ruiz, Alicia R. Gable, Edward H. Kaplan, Michael A. Stoto, Harvey V. Fineberg, and James Trussell. Washington, DC: National Academy Press, 2001. Copyright © 2001 by the National Academy of Sciences. Reproduced by permission of the publisher.

vaccines prior to use in humans; available models are either too costly or inadequately mimic human infection and the disease processes. Second, the nature of the immune response needed to prevent HIV is unknown, as there have been no cases of recovery that can be studied. Third, the vaccines under development are primarily oriented toward clade B, the strain of the virus that is most common in wealthier nations. Given the significant genetic diversity among clades, it is uncertain whether a vaccine that proves effective for one clade would provide protection against different viral subtypes.

Vaccine research and development is considered commercially very risky.

Economic incentives to encourage private sector investment in HIV vaccine research also are lacking due to factors such as the general underconsumption of vaccines (particularly by developing nations with limited health care resources) and the unwillingness of private industries to pursue research and development opportunities that are socially valuable or which contribute to the international public good. Vaccine research and development is considered commercially very risky; it is expensive and time consuming, taking approximately 10–12 years to develop a new product and bring it to market. Further, vaccine research and development often does not yield a significant financial return on investment, as it often takes more than a decade for companies to recover their research and development costs for a new vaccine. Although private investment in vaccine development has improved, most companies have relegated such work to a lower priority due to the higher demand and market for therapeutic drugs (e.g., antiretrovirals), as well as the length of time required for product development, testing, and approval. As a result, most of the investments in HIV vaccine research have come from the public sector. The International AIDS Vaccine Initiative (IAVI) and other organizations are currently spearheading efforts to encourage more private sector investment in vaccine research and development.

Vaccine trials underway

Nevertheless, some candidate vaccines have shown promise in protecting against HIV infection and have been tested in humans. Trials of vaccines derived from viral subunits (i.e., genetically engineered proteins of HIV) suggest that they provide only a limited protective response. However, in recognition of the fact that a vaccine that generates any amount of protective response may help in curtailing the epidemic in the developing world, where it is most acute, efficacy trials of subunit vaccines are currently under way in Thailand and Uganda. Vaccine trials using live attenuated [less deadly] HIV are being seriously considered, but have not yet been conducted in humans due to safety concerns. Other vaccine strategies, including using live virus vector and DNA vaccines, are currently being investigated. Issues of greatest concern in vaccine trials include the safety and immunogenicity of vaccines, their effectiveness against infection and disease resulting from different modes of transmission, and the permanence of the protective response.

Similarly, there is concern that availability of a vaccine that is even partially effective could contribute to resurgences in risk behaviors. To curb the potential adverse effects, prior to vaccine clinical trials or immunization programs, prevention and education programs must be implemented and sustained to ensure that behaviors to prevent HIV transmission are continued. Even when a vaccine is available, it would be important to maintain emphasis on and invest in other prevention efforts (e.g., counseling and testing, risk reduction education, provision of barrier methods, etc.) that could be provided simultaneously with a vaccine to prevent other sexually transmitted infections or unwanted pregnancies.

The characteristics of the virus, including its high mutability, its different modes of transmission, and the differing biological characteristics of its affected populations make the development of a universally effective vaccine problematic. Given these factors, it will be essential to discourage perceptions that a vaccine is a "magic bullet" that will forever eliminate HIV.

14

Reducing Poverty Can Reduce AIDS in Developing Countries

Robert Hecht, Olusoji Adeyi, and Iris Semini

Robert Hecht is senior adviser to the vice president for Human Development at the World Bank and has served as associate director of the Joint United Nations Program on HIV/AIDS (UNAIDS). Olusoji Adeyi is a senior health specialist for HIV/AIDS in the Europe and Central Asia Region of the World Bank. Iris Semini is technical officer on poverty, debt, and AIDS at UNAIDS.

There is growing global recognition that AIDS is exacerbated by poverty and, in turn, further impoverishes poor nations. Indeed, many analysts are realizing that as more people in developing countries die of AIDS, the fewer workers there are to contribute to the economy and the less able such nations become to finance strategies to fight AIDS. As a result of this new awareness, policymakers are developing new tools to fight AIDS, such as the Poverty Reduction Strategy Paper (PRSP). PRSPs assist poor nations who are experiencing high rates of AIDS cases. Participating low-income countries prepare PRSP documents to describe the policies and programs they expect to implement to reduce their country's poverty and outline how much money they will need to implement them. Forty low-income countries have taken the first steps in using PRSPs with varying degrees of success. Tools such as PRSPs can help reduce poverty and, in consequence, slow the transmission of AIDS.

AIDS is not just a health issue but a development problem that must be addressed at the global level. As countries increasingly recognize the need to incorporate strategies for tackling AIDS in their national policy frameworks, they are discovering important new weapons—notably national poverty reduction plans—that were not available even two years ago. In [2001 and 2002], development thinking has undergone a major shift, from viewing AIDS as purely a health issue to acknowledging that it must be tackled as part of a broader development agenda. There is evidence of this new approach, referred to as "mainstreaming," at the highest levels of development policy and assistance. At a meeting of the Development Committee of the World Bank and the International Monetary Fund (IMF) April 2001, ministers called for focusing on HIV/AIDS in development policies and increasing assistance to affected countries. Developing countries themselves have announced their intention of making AIDS a mainstream issue, most visibly in June 2001 during the United Nations General Assembly Special Session on HIV/AIDS.

Why is this shift in thinking so important? HIV/AIDS takes a heavy toll, both economic and human, as it undermines productivity, security, education, health care, civil service systems, social cohesion, and political stability. It is shortening the life expectancy of working-age adults, dramatically increasing the numbers of infant and child deaths, shrinking the workforce, creating tens of millions of orphans, widening the gap between rich and poor, and reversing development gains. Since the onset of the epidemic, almost 22 million people worldwide have died of AIDS, and another 36 million people are living with the HIV virus. In Africa alone, 12 million men, women, and children—more than the entire population of Belgium—have died to date.

Developing countries that do not, or cannot, protect human capital—the education and skills embodied in people that enable them to increase their future incomes—will not be able to participate fully in the global economy, much less take advantage of the opportunities it affords. Smallholder farm families in Zimbabwe experience a 40–60 percent fall in the production of maize, peanuts, and cotton after suffering an AIDS death. Children who lose a parent to AIDS in rural Tanzania are about 50 percent more likely to be malnourished than children from families with both parents living. Data from over 15 African and Latin American countries also show that children who lose both parents to AIDS are much less likely to continue attending school. A recent World Bank study estimates that Africa's income growth per capita is being reduced by about 0.7 percent a year because of HIV/AIDS.

HIV/AIDS takes a heavy toll, both economic and human, as it undermines productivity, security, education, healthcare, civil service systems, social cohesion, and political stability.

Moreover, although AIDS is not exclusively a disease of the poor, much evidence suggests that certain poor groups run a disproportionately greater risk of becoming infected with the HIV virus. In many countries, infections are heavily concentrated among injecting drug users and their partners and among commercial sex workers, most of whom are poor. Even in Africa, where the epidemic is now widespread, it appears that HIV infection rates are starting to fall among more educated women while continuing to rise among those with little or no schooling.

Fortunately, policymakers now have at their disposal a new tool—the

Poverty Reduction Strategy Paper (PRSP)—that greatly facilitates mainstreaming the fight against HIV/AIDS. The PRSP, which sets out a country's approach to poverty reduction, can be used by the donor community as a framework for technical and financial support. Moreover, its usefulness has been dramatically enhanced in recent years by the availability of debt relief for the world's poorest countries.

Poverty reduction tool

What exactly are PRSPs? They are documents in which low-income countries describe the policies and programs they expect to put in place to promote growth and reduce poverty, the associated external financing needs, and major sources of financing. Each country prepares its own PRSP with input from domestic stakeholders and external development partners.

To be effective, a country's poverty reduction strategy should be led by the country itself; aim for faster economic growth that specifically addresses the needs of the poor; reflect a comprehensive understanding of poverty and its determinants; help identify the public actions that have the greatest impact on poverty; and establish outcome indicators that are set and monitored by the government, with domestic and external input.

Policymakers now have at their disposal a new tool—the Poverty Reduction Strategy Paper (PRSP)— that greatly facilitates mainstreaming the fight against HIV/AIDS.

Partly to qualify for debt relief under the Heavily Indebted Poor Countries (HIPC) Initiative, launched by the IMF and the World Bank in 1996, about 40 low-income countries took the first steps toward elaborating a full PRSP during 2000–01 by preparing an interim PRSP in which they began to analyze the extent and causes of poverty and the main actions needed to combat it, and outlined the process for producing a full strategy. By the end of 2001, 8 countries had completed and published full PRSPs, and many others were working to complete their full PRSPs.

Recently, the UNAIDS Secretariat reviewed the first generation of 25 full and interim PRSPs prepared by sub-Saharan African countries to get a sense of how well they are dealing with HIV/AIDS. The review was based on four criteria: (1) analysis of the relationship between AIDS and poverty; (2) inclusion of the main strategies from the country's national AIDS plan; (3) use of medium-term AIDS prevention and care goals and indicators for monitoring poverty; and (4) incorporation of monitorable short-term actions to fight HIV/AIDS.

What was the verdict? The initial signs were promising, but far more could be done to fully exploit the potential of PRSPs. The countries rated highest on inclusion in the PRSPs of approaches for fighting AIDS drawn from their national AIDS plans. Their analysis of the relationship between AIDS and poverty was generally weak, however, even in countries where research has been done on the social and economic impact of the epidemic. The elaboration of short-term actions and medium-term goals on

AIDS was also generally weak or even nonexistent. The review did not examine the quality of national and local participation.

Clearly, future PRSPs can provide a sounder basis for making decisions about AIDS funding if they pay more attention to the links between AIDS and poverty. Poverty strategies can draw on the growing evidence of the impact of HIV illness and AIDS deaths on household production and incomes, school attendance, and child nutrition. In addition, the main AIDS prevention and care strategies need to be more clearly defined, for example, working through schools and peer counselors to change the sexual behaviors of young people and using nongovernmental organizations (NGOs) to reach commercial sex workers and their clients with information, condoms, and care for other sexually transmitted infections. The identification of medium-term AIDS goals and indicators in each country should build on the targets already agreed upon as part of the Millennium Development Goals [the United Nation's World-wide goals to be reached by 2015], including reducing the incidence of new HIV infections among 15–24-year-olds and of infections transmitted from pregnant women to their unborn children.

Uganda, one of Africa's worst-affected countries, has become the continent's success story and can serve as a model for others. It has succeeded in reducing the HIV prevalence rate in young women from 25 percent in 1992 to 8 percent today. Uganda's PRSP describes the impoverishing effects of AIDS on women, orphans, and households. It highlights strategies for reducing new HIV infections, mitigating the health and socioeconomic effects of the epidemic, and improving Uganda's capacity to respond to the problem. The PRSP then sets an overall target for reducing HIV prevalence in the adult population, as well as more detailed objectives and targets, such as reducing violence against women and improving access to AIDS counseling, care, and social support.

15

Developing Countries Need to Reduce Risky Behavior to Prevent AIDS

Martha Ainsworth

Martha Ainsworth is a senior economist in the Development Research Group of the World Bank and is coauthor of Confronting AIDS: Public Priorities in a Global Epidemic.

Changing individual behavior is an important factor in arresting the spread of the AIDS epidemic in developing countries. Because human behavior plays a critical role in the transmission of the AIDS virus, preventive measures such as condom use and avoiding needle sharing must be encouraged among people most likely to spread the disease. Helping to implement these preventive measures must be a high priority for the governments of developing countries, where individuals do not have the education or resources to fight the disease. Furthermore, governments can assist people engaging in high-risk behavior by lowering the costs of safer behavior and raising the costs of risky behavior.

Public policy has proved to be an effective weapon in containing the HIV/AIDS epidemic. Governments can have the greatest impact by providing incentives for those most likely to spread HIV to adopt safer behavior.

No cure has yet been found for the virus that causes AIDS, and an effective vaccine is still far off. The key to arresting the AIDS epidemic in developing countries is preventing HIV infection by changing individual behavior. What actions can be taken to encourage such change, and to which of these should governments give priority?

Behavior change is key

The biological characteristics of HIV determine, to some extent, the rate at which it spreads, but human behavior plays a critical role in transmis-

Martha Ainsworth, "Setting Government Priorities in Preventing HIV/AIDS," *Finance & Development,* vol. 35, March 1998, p. 18. Copyright © 1998 by *Finance & Development.* Reproduced by permission.

sion. People who have many sexual partners and do not use condoms, and people who inject drugs and share unsterilized injecting equipment have the greatest risk of contracting HIV and unknowingly infecting others. Typically, the virus first spreads quickly in a series of small epidemics among those with the riskiest behavior; it then spreads more slowly from them to lower-risk individuals in the population at large. How quickly and extensively an HIV/AIDS epidemic spreads in a given population depends largely on the extent to which people with many sexual partners mix with people with fewer partners.

The World Bank research report *Confronting AIDS: Public Priorities in a Global Epidemic* finds that people who engage in high-risk behavior do act to reduce their risk of contracting and spreading HIV when they have the knowledge and means to do so and a supportive community. The report highlights three strategies to reduce risky behavior: providing information, lowering the costs of safer behavior, and raising the costs of risky behavior.

Knowledge of how extensive HIV infection is in one's community, how the virus is transmitted, and how to avoid contracting it will induce some people to behave more safely—for example, by using condoms, reducing the number of sexual partners, sterilizing injecting equipment, or avoiding needle sharing. In Thailand, the announcement in 1989 that 44 percent of sex workers in the northern city of Chiang Mai were infected with HIV is believed to have contributed to the growing use of condoms, even before the launching of large-scale government programs. Condom use by young adults in the United States doubled in the mid-to-late 1980s because of growing awareness of the risk of contracting HIV.

But knowledge alone is unlikely to change individual behavior enough to stop the HIV/AIDS epidemic. Many of the individuals who engage in high-risk behavior are likely to make decisions based on what they perceive to be their own risk of contracting HIV, while ignoring the risks to which their actions expose others. Even when considering their own risk of infection, many people persist in risky behavior because the costs of safer behavior are clear and immediate, while the benefits are uncertain and distant.

Lowering the costs of condom use and safe injecting behavior

Condoms are highly effective in preventing HIV transmission, but they entail costs—not only the money and time spent buying condoms, but potential inconvenience and embarrassment and, for some people, reduced pleasure. Reducing these costs will encourage more people to use condoms and lead to lower rates of HIV transmission. In Kinshasa, Democratic Republic of Congo, a program that offered sex workers free condoms, treatment for other sexually transmitted diseases, counseling, and group discussions had impressive results. A mere 11 percent of the sex workers had used condoms on an "occasional" basis before the program; afterwards, more than two-thirds reported using condoms on a "consistent" basis. The incidence of HIV—the number of new cases over time—dropped by two-thirds. At the same time, mass marketing of highly subsidized condoms—known as "social marketing"—in Kinshasa increased the willingness of clients to use them. Sixty developing countries now have condom social marketing programs, both for the prevention of sexually transmitted diseases and HIV infection and for family planning.

Injecting drug users face substantial costs in adopting safer behavior. For people who are truly addicted, drug treatment programs are often difficult to get into and painful to go through; 70–80 percent of those treated typically resume drug use within a year or two of completing treatment. The scarcity of sterile injecting equipment is one of the most important reasons why injecting drug users share needles and syringes, spreading HIV and other blood-borne diseases. The availability of sterile injecting equipment is highly restricted in many countries; possession of it may be illegal and lead to imprisonment.

The key to arresting the AIDS epidemic in developing countries is preventing HIV infection by changing individual behavior.

"Harm-reduction" programs reduce these costs and increase safe injecting behavior among people who cannot stop injecting drugs. They include such measures as legalization of over-the-counter purchase of needles and syringes, bleach distribution, needle exchange, outreach by peer educators, and referral for drug treatment. Needle exchange programs, which provide new, sterile injecting equipment in exchange for used syringes, reduce needle sharing and remove contaminated needles from circulation. Such programs are credited with keeping HIV infection levels below 5 percent among injecting drug users in cities like Glasgow, Scotland, and Tacoma, United States, even as infection rates have soared to 40 percent or more in neighboring cities. In Kathmandu, Nepal, a program offering needle exchange, bleach, education, and health care to injecting drug users lowered the frequency of injection by one-third and the number of unsafe injections by one-half; HIV prevalence has remained low—less than 2 percent of injecting drug users—while the prevalence of HIV among injecting drug users in India and Myanmar has soared to 60 percent or more. Evaluations of these programs find no evidence that they encourage people to start injecting drugs, but there is substantial evidence that they reduce the types of behavior that spread HIV.

Raising the costs of risky behavior

An alternative strategy to reduce risky behavior is to make it illegal, more difficult, or costlier, for example, by enforcing laws against commercial sex or drug use, or by reducing the drug supply. Such a strategy may appeal to many people because both prostitution and the use of addictive drugs have substantial negative externalities for the rest of society—the spread of sexually transmitted and blood-borne diseases, higher crime rates, and increased expenditures on law enforcement and incarceration. However, attempts to prohibit or regulate these behaviors are costly and difficult to enforce, and rarely succeed in either eliminating or controlling them. Prohibition may discourage some people but merely drives others "underground," where it is harder for public health programs to reach them, or it may simply "rearrange" the problem. When Singapore attempted to eradicate prostitution by closing "red-light" districts, brothels appeared in residential areas. Legalizing prostitution makes the legal segment of the commercial sex market easier to reach and regulate, but it tends to raise prices for the regulated sexual services, giving rise to a lower-cost parallel market of unregulated sex workers who are harder to reach. When prostitution was officially regulated in Melbourne, Australia, the number of brothels declined by two-thirds; the price of sex in brothels rose; and the number of lower-priced "streetwalkers" increased.

Similarly, attempts to restrict the supply of drugs or to put drug addicts in prison may not only fail to slow the rate of HIV transmission but may have the opposite effect. Efforts to control opium smoking in Bangkok and Calcutta induced addicts to switch from smoking to injecting heroin, increasing the risk of HIV transmission. The threat of imprisonment is notoriously ineffective in getting injecting drug users to quit; HIV spreads very rapidly among prisoners who continue to inject drugs using shared, improvised equipment, like ballpoint pens and rubber tubing, which are hard to sterilize.

It is difficult to measure the impact on HIV transmission of raising the costs of risky behavior because such behavior is often clandestine. Commercial sex or injecting drugs per se do not spread HIV—the failure to use condoms and the sharing of unsterilized needles and syringes do. Given the high costs of enforcement, the possibility that unsafe behavior may actually increase as a result of prohibitions, and evidence that people adopt safer behavior when the incentives are right, programs that reduce the costs of safer behavior are likely to be more cost effective in preventing HIV transmission.

Government priorities

Given the enormous consequences of HIV/AIDS, few people would debate the need for developing country governments to take action to curb the epidemic. But these governments are faced with numerous pressing demands and a shortage of funds. Which activities should receive priority?

Governments have two key responsibilities in preventing the spread of HIV/AIDS: reducing the negative externalities of high-risk behavior and producing public goods. Some societies will want to do more than this and may have the money to do so. But these two activities, which are essential for stopping the epidemic, are priorities for all governments because, without government action, private individuals and firms will not have the incentives to do what is necessary. Governments also have a responsibility to protect the poor, who will best be served in most countries by measures that prevent infection among high-risk individuals.

Preventing HIV among those most likely to spread it

Because of the negative externalities of high-risk behavior, governments must ensure effective prevention efforts among people most likely to contract and spread HIV. Preventive measures among people with many sexual partners, for example, will do more to protect those in the general population from infection than will preventive measures among people who have few sexual partners. A program for sex workers in Nairobi, Kenya, vividly illustrates this point. By treating the other sexually transmitted diseases of 500 sex workers and increasing their condom use to 80 percent, the program prevented 10,000 HIV infections a year among their clients, and the clients' spouses and other partners. In contrast, had condom use been raised to 80 percent of an equal number of men taken at random from the same community, fewer than 100 infections a year would have been prevented.

Knowledge of how extensive HIV infection is in one's community . . . and how to avoid contracting it will induce some people to behave more safely.

In setting priorities, therefore, prevention measures should first focus on prevention among people with the greatest risk of transmitting HIV. As additional resources become available, prevention efforts can be extended progressively to people who are less likely to spread the virus.

Simulations show that in countries where HIV infection levels are low, prevention of transmission among those with the very riskiest behavior may be sufficient to prevent a widespread epidemic. Even in countries where HIV is already widespread, it is likely to be the most cost-effective strategy in curbing the spread of HIV, although a much larger group must be covered to bring infection levels down quickly.

Directly or indirectly, governments of developing countries can successfully implement such programs on a wide scale. In Thailand, a multi-faceted program increased condom use in brothels to more than 90 percent of sex workers. At the same time, the number of patients with other sexually transmitted diseases, like gonorrhea and syphilis, has dropped by 90 percent. HIV infection among young army conscripts peaked at 4 percent in 1993; since then it has declined by more than half. Other countries, like Brazil and India, have succeeded in reaching those with the highest-risk behavior by enlisting nongovernmental organizations, which often have greater flexibility and more access to intended program participants, to implement programs.

Despite these successes, available evidence suggests that most countries have not reached the majority of people with the riskiest behavior.

• In surveys in seven African countries hard-hit by the epidemic, respondents were asked how they could protect themselves from getting AIDS. Of the respondents who had recently had a casual sexual partner, only 40–70 percent named condom use as a means of protection.

• People in the military are thought to have a high risk of contracting and spreading HIV because they are often stationed away from their families. A study of HIV/AIDS prevention measures in the militaries of 50 industrial and developing countries found that one-fifth of the militaries did not distribute condoms and that most of the others offered condoms free of charge but only on request.

• A survey of UNAIDS (Joint United Nations Programme on HIV/AIDS) Country Programme Advisers for 32 developing countries found that public and private HIV prevention efforts rarely reached even half of the groups with high-risk behavior. In fact, many governments have impeded prevention efforts from reaching injecting drug users and men who have sex with men.

Governments also need to invest in public goods essential to the control of HIV: monitoring infection and behavior, providing information on how HIV can be transmitted and prevented, and evaluating the costs and effects of different approaches. Likewise, bilateral and multilateral donors have a responsibility to invest in information that is an "international" public good: medical research on a vaccine that can be effective in developing countries; low-cost, effective treatments for AIDS in low-income countries; and evaluation of the cost-effectiveness of behavioral and medical interventions in the field.

The future of the epidemic is not carved in stone.
Action now can save millions of lives.

The available evidence suggests that, for prevention efforts to succeed, many countries need to invest in information about the types and distribution of risky behavior in the population and, among those with risky behavior, the prevalence of HIV infection. However, fewer than 20 developing countries have carried out sexual behavior surveys. As recently as 1995, one-fourth of all developing countries had not yet initiated systematic monitoring of HIV prevalence. More than one-third of the 123 countries studied for *Confronting AIDS* had no information on HIV prevalence in populations with high-risk behavior during the past five years. Equally critical, very few studies have attempted to measure both the costs and effects of programs and almost none have included the prevention of secondary infections as one of the benefits.

The need to act now

Epidemiological models predict that between 1996 and 2001, 10 million to 30 million people in developing countries will become infected with HIV. But the future of the epidemic is not carved in stone. Action now can save millions of lives. *Confronting AIDS* classifies developing countries by the extent to which HIV has spread among people with the riskiest behavior and from them to the general population.

• 2.3 billion people (half of the population of the developing world) live in areas with "nascent" epidemics—that is, HIV has infected fewer than 5 percent of people presumed to have high-risk behavior. Bangladesh, Indonesia, the Philippines, and most countries of the former Soviet Union, as well as vast areas of China and India, fall into this category. Immediate action to prevent infection in the groups with the highest risk can avert a widespread epidemic.

• 1.6 billion people live in countries with "concentrated" epidemics—that is, more than 5 percent of the highest-risk individuals have been infected with HIV but the infection rate for the rest of the population is still low. Most of Indochina, Latin America, and West Africa, as well as Yunnan Province of China and about half of India have concentrated epidemics. Thailand's experience shows that concerted action focused on people with the riskiest behavior can have immediate impacts, even in a concentrated epidemic.

• About 250 million people live in countries with "generalized" epidemics. The rate of HIV infection in these countries is high in the groups with the riskiest behavior, and 5 percent or more of the women visiting antenatal clinics are infected, indicating that HIV has spread widely in the general population. Most countries in eastern and southern Africa, a few West African countries, and Guyana and Haiti fall into this category. These countries must cope with the impact of severe AIDS epidemics while maintaining strong prevention programs, especially among those most likely to spread the virus.

Mobilizing political support

Virtually every country that is confronting a severe AIDS epidemic once claimed: "It can't happen here." Initially, policymakers denied that the types of behaviors responsible for the transmission of the virus existed in their culture and blamed foreigners. But in each and every case they have been wrong.

It is not difficult to understand why denial is such a common response. When only a few people are sick, policymakers and the public have difficulty grasping the urgency of preventive measures; the programs needed to prevent transmission of the virus are often controversial; and other development problems seem more pressing. Unfortunately, denial robs society of precious time during which early and focused action could avert an epidemic. Because a long asymptomatic period—lasting 8–10 years—usually follows infection with HIV, by the time a significant number of AIDS cases appear and the public awakens to the threat of HIV/AIDS, many people will have been infected. At that point, preventing an epidemic is costlier and more difficult.

Programs that aim to prevent HIV among those with the riskiest behavior are controversial but they save lives. Without them, the epidemic cannot be stopped. Emotional responses are not a good guide to dealing with this public health problem. The public needs to understand that the most effective way of preventing an epidemic that could eventually affect all of us in some way is to encourage those most likely to contract and spread HIV to adopt safer behavior. Stigmatization of these individuals and discrimination against them are counterproductive. Only by facing these difficult issues will developing countries succeed in blunting the tragic impact of AIDS.

Organizations and Websites

The editors have compiled the following list of organizations concerned with the issues debated in this book. The descriptions are derived from materials provided by the organizations. All have publications or information available for interested readers. The list was compiled on the date of publication of the present volume; names, addresses, phone and fax numbers, and e-mail addresses may change. Be aware that many organizations take several weeks or longer to respond to inquiries, so allow as much time as possible.

AIDS Vaccine Advocacy Coalition (AVAC)
101 West 23rd St., #2227, New York, NY 10011
(212) 367-1084
e-mail: avac@avac.org • website: www.avac.org

AVAC is a community- and consumer-based organization founded in 1995 to accelerate the ethical development and global delivery of vaccines against HIV/AIDS. The organization provides independent analysis, policy advocacy, public education, and mobilization to enhance AIDS research and development, it also provides the AVAC Update Newsletter Handbook, "Community Perspective on Participation in Research, Advocacy, and Progress."

The Beyond Awareness Campaign
+27 11 880-8868
e-mail: actpso@effectcompany.com • website: www.aidsinfo.co.za

The Beyond Awareness Campaign is a project of the HIV/AIDS and STD (sexually transmitted diseases) Directorate of the South African Department of Health. The site details a wide range of communications activities undertaken as part of a national campaign. Many useful documents that are relevant in Africa and internationally can be downloaded.

The Global AIDS Interfaith Alliance (GAIA)
The Presidio of San Francisco, PO Box 29110, San Francisco, CA 94129-0110
(415) 461-7196 • fax: (415) 461-9681
e-mail: info@thegaia.org • website: www.thegaia.org

GAIA is a nonprofit organization composed of top AIDS researchers and doctors, religious leaders, concerned benefactors, and African medical officials, most of whom are associated with religiously based clinics and hospitals. The organization was founded in June 2000 to stop the transmission of HIV from mothers to infants in sub-Saharan Africa. The present program is concerned with infrastructure development, training of prevention educators, and personnel to conduct HIV testing and counseling. It also emphasizes the modification of values, structures, and practices that predispose women and girls to higher HIV infection rates than men, that stigmatize ill persons, and that contribute to public denial. GAIA brochure offers news and updates.

Global Health Council
20 Palmer Ct., White River Junction, VT 05001
(802) 649-1340 • fax: (802) 649-1396
e-mail: ghc@globalhealth.org • website: www.globalhealth.org

The Global Health Council is a U.S.-based, nonprofit membership organization that was created in 1972 to identify priority health problems and to report on them to the U.S. public, Congress, international and domestic government agencies, academic institutions, and the global health community. Its global AIDS program focuses on facilitating, networking, and information exchange with a special emphasis on developing world networking. The Global Health Council's online publications include Global AIDSLink, Global HealthLink, the 2002–2003 Global AIDS Directory, and a newsletter.

Health GAP Coalition
511 E. Fifth St. #4, New York, NY 10009
(212) 674-9598 • fax: (212) 208-4533
e-mail: info@healthgap.org • website: www.healthgap.org

The Health GAP Coalition is one of the many groups involved in the protests regarding AIDS drug access and U.S. trade policy. The website contains links and information on efforts to secure international treatment access as well as instructions for subscribing to the Health GAP e-mail discussion list and the Treatment Access list.The Health GAP Coalition offers numerous papers and reports.

International AIDS Vaccine Initiative (IAVI)
110 William St., New York, NY 10038
(212) 847-1111 • fax: (212) 847-1112
e-mail: info@iavi.org • website: www.iavi.org

IAVI is a global organization working to speed the development and distribution of preventive AIDS vaccines. IAVI's work focuses on mobilizing support through advocacy and education, acceleration of scientific progress, encouraging industrial participation in AIDS vaccine development, and assuring global access to the vaccines. IAVI publishes fact sheets and policy papers about the organization's programs and a variety of issues concerning AIDS vaccine development.

International Association of Physicians in AIDS Care (IAPAC)
33 N. La Salle St., Suite 1700, Chicago, IL 60602
(312) 795-4930 • fax: (312) 795-4938
e-mail: iapac@iapac.org • website: www.iapac.org

This organization serves as a resource and as a public service for physicians and other health care professionals, nongovernmental and governmental agencies, communities of faith, and others throughout the world who care for and about the hundreds of millions of children, women, and men infected and affected by the life-threatening infectious diseases, poverty, and dehumanization. IAPAC offers HIV/AIDS stories from across the Internet and gives news updates.

International Council of AIDS Services Organizations (ICASO)
399 Church St. 4th Fl., Toronto ON M5B ZJ6, Canada
(416) 340-2437 • fax: (416) 340-8224
website: www.icaso.org

ICASO is a network of community-based AIDS organizations that brings together all those groups throughout the world that have arisen out of community efforts to control the spread and impact of HIV/AIDS. It recognizes human rights as being central to an intelligent public health stategy to combat the epidemic. The ICASO network is an interactive global focus point in the international HIV/AIDS world, gathering and disseminating information and analysis on key issues. ICASO provides the ICASO Newsletter including *HIV/AIDS and Human Rights—Stories from the Frontlines*, and the ICASO Networking Guide.

Médecins sans Frontières (MSF) Doctors Without Borders
Rue du Lac 12, PO Box 6090 CH-1211, Geneva 6, Switzerland
(4122) 849-8407 • fax: (4122) 849-8404
e-mail: davidberman@geneva.msf.org • website: www.accessmed-msf.org

MSF is an international humanitarian aid organization that provides emergency medical assistance to populations in danger in more than eighty countries. MSF seeks to raise awareness of crisis situations and speaks out about the plight of populations in danger. MSF issues reports and publications on diseases, globalization, overcoming barriers, and specific medicinal issues, and research and development.

UNAIDS
20 Ave. Appia, CH-1211, Geneva 27, Switzerland
(4122) 791-3666 • fax: (4122) 791-4187
website: www.unaids.org

UNAIDS is a joint UN program on HIV/AIDS created by the combination of six organizations. UNAIDS is a leading advocate for worldwide action against HIV/AIDS, and the global mission of UNAIDS is to lead, strengthen, and support an expanded response to the AIDS epidemic that will prevent the spread of HIV, provide care and support for those infected and affected by AIDS, and alleviate the socioeconomic and human impact of the epidemic. UNAIDS has many publications including *HIV/AIDS Human Resources and Sustainable Development, Global HIV/AIDS Epidemic 2002–2003—A Conceptual Framework and Basis for Action,* and *Young People and HIV/AIDS: Opportunity in Crisis.*

The World Health Organization (WHO)
2 United Nations Plaza, DC-2 Bldg., Rms. 0956 to 0976, New York, NY 10017
(212) 963-4388 • fax: (212) 223-2920
website: www.who.int

WHO is a UN specialized agency for health whose objective is the attainment of the highest possible level of heatlh by all peoples. WHO is governed by 191 member states through the World Health Assembly. Its website provides links to descriptions of activities, reports, news, and events as well as contacts in the various WHO programs on the topic of AIDS. WHO publishes the *Bulletin of World Health Organization, World Health Report,* and *WHO Drug Information.*

Youth Against AIDS
+44 20 7278-7844 • fax: +44 87 0120-9813
e-mail: interact@worldvoices.org • website: http://www.worldvoices.org/aids

Youth Against AIDS is an organization of African youth whose goal is to spread an awareness of AIDS and to get their voices and views heard, both in Africa and internationally.

Additional Internet Resources

AIDS Channel
website: www.aidschannel.org
This website features issues relating to HIV/AIDS and brings together information and resources from civil society organizations, government and research institutions, media, and others working in the field.

AIDS Education Global Information System (AEGIS)
website: www.aegis.org
AEGIS is a grassroots effort to accumulate information and knowledge about AIDS. The site offers fact sheets, publications, a law library, reference material, and links.

AIDSnews.org
website: www.aidsnews.org
This website provides lists of useful Internet links and resources as well as AIDS databases.

AIDSonline.com
website: www.aidsonline.com
AIDSonline.com is the journal of the International AIDS Society and provides information on AIDS as well as resources and links to other AIDS sites.

AIDS.org
website: www.aids.org/index.html
AIDS.org provides online AIDS education and ways for people to communicate with each other, sharing HIV and AIDS information. It features AIDS fact sheets, an AIDS bookstore with online reviews of books about HIV and AIDS, and daily news about AIDS.

The Body
website: www.thebody.com
A service of Body Health Resources Corporation, this site has information on more than 550 topics, including AIDS basics, a "visual aids" gallery, treatment information, policy and activism, and an "ask the experts" section.

British HIV Association and National AIDS Manual
website: www.aidsmap.com
This site offers basic information on HIV and AIDS, HIV/AIDS statistics worldwide, new drugs available, and an extensive listing of international HIV/AIDS service agencies.

National Pediatric and Family HIV Resources Center
website: www.pedhivaids.org
This website features AIDS news and events, educational material, links to AIDS-related sites, questions and answers, and global AIDS information.

Nigeria-AIDS.org
website: www.nigeria-aids.org
Nigeria-AIDS.org is an information source on HIV/AIDS in Nigeria and the West African subregion. It is the website of Journalists Against AIDS Nigeria, the award-winning media-based nongovernmental HIV/AIDS advocacy organization.

Bibliography

Books

Tony Barnett and Alan Whiteside	*AIDS in the Twenty-First Century: Disease and Globilization.* New York: Palgrave Macmillan, 2002.
Abbey Begun, Jacquelyn F. Quiram, and Nancy R. Jacobs, eds.	*AIDS.* Wylie, TX: Information Plus, 1998.
Karen Bellenir	*AIDS Sourcebook.* Detroit: Omnigraphics, 1999.
Jon Cohen	*Shots in the Dark.* New York: WW. Norton, 2001.
Michael A. DiSpezio	*The Science, Spread, and Therapy of HIV Disease: Everything You Need to Know, but Had No Idea Who to Ask.* Shrewsbury, MA: ATL Press, 1998.
Hung Fan	*AIDS: Science and Society.* Boston: Jones and Bartlett, 2000.
Emma Guest	*Children of AIDS: Africa's Orphan Crisis.* Sterling, VA: Pluto Press, 2001.
Edward Hooper	*The River: A Journey to the Source of HIV and AIDS.* Boston: Little, Brown and Co., 1999.
Janet Majure	*AIDS.* Springfield, NJ: Enslow Publishers, 1998.
Jonathan M. Mann and Daniel J.M. Tarantola, eds.	*AIDS in the World II: Global Dimensions, Social Roots, and Responses.* New York: Oxford University Press, 1996.
Stephanie Marcus	*HIV/AIDS.* Washington, DC: Library of Congress, 1998.
Luc Montagnier	*Virus: The Co-Discoverer of HIV Tracks Its Rampage and Charts the Future.* New York: WW. Norton, 2000.
Japheth Ng'weshemi	*HIV Prevention and AIDS Care in Africa.* Amsterdam: Royal Tropical Institute, 1997.
Gary Null	*AIDS: A Second Opinion.* New York: Seven Stories Press, 2001.
Kenneth L. Packer	*HIV Infection: The Facts You Need to Know.* New York: Franklin Watts, 1998.
Tamara L. Roleff and Charles P. Cozic, eds.	*AIDS: Opposing Viewpoints.* San Diego, CA: Greenhaven Press, 1998.
Barry D. Schoub	*AIDS and HIV in Perspective.* Cambridge: Cambridge University Press, 1999.
Randy Shilts	*And the Band Played On: Politics, People, and the AIDS Epidemic.* New York: St. Martin's Press, 2000.

Alvin Silverstein	*AIDS: An All About Guide for Young Adults.* Springfield, NJ: Enslow Publishers, 1999.
Raymond A. Smith, ed.	*Encyclopedia of AIDS.* New York: Penguin, 2001.
Gerald J. Stine	*AIDS Update.* Upper Saddle River, NJ: Prentice-Hall, 2002.
Barbara Taylor	*Everything You Need to Know About AIDS.* New York: Rosen Publishing Group, 1998.
Susan Taylor-Brown and Alejandro Garcia, eds.	*HIV Affected and Vulnerable Youth: Prevention Issues and Approaches.* Binghamton, NY: Haworth, 2001.
Douglas Webb	*HIV and AIDS in Africa.* Sterling, VA: Pluto Press, 1997.
Flossie Wong-Staal and Robert C. Gallo, eds.	*AIDS Vaccine Research.* New York: Marcel Dekker, 2002.

Periodicals

Asian Economic News (Beijing)	"Number of HIV/AIDS Patients Increases in China," October 2001.
Tim Batchelder	"The Anthropology of HIV-AIDS," *Townsend Letter for Doctors and Patients*, April 2002.
Gary S. Becker	"How to Get AIDS Drugs to Africa," *Business Week*, April 23, 2001.
Ken Bluestone	"Safeguarding Developing Countries' Rights to Affordable Medicines for HIV/AIDS: How Effective Are International Trade Rules?" *Tropical Medicine and International Health*, March 2001.
Salih Booker and William Minter	"Global Apartheid," *Nation*, July 2001.
James Cochrane	"Narrowing the Gap: Access to HIV Treatments in Developing Countries," *Journal of Medical Ethics*, February 2000.
Jon Cohen	"AIDS Vaccines Show Promise After Years of Frustration," *Science*, March 2, 2001.
Kevin De Cock and Robert S. Janssen	"An Unequal Epidemic in an Unequal World," *Journal of the American Medical Association*, July 2002.
Josie Glausiusz	"The Chasm in Care," *Discover*, January 1999.
Merrill Goozner	"Third World Battles for AIDS Drugs," *Chicago Tribune*, April 28, 1999.
Alison D. Grant and Kevin De Cock	"HIV Infection and AIDS in the Developing World," *British Medical Journal*, June 2001.
Pranay B. Gupte	"Annan's AIDS Crusade," *Nation*, July 2001.
Prabhat Jha	"Reducing HIV Transmission in Developing Countries," *Science*, April 2001.

Peter R. Lamptey   "Reducing Heterosexual Transmisson of HIV in Poor
                          Countries," *British Medical Journal*, January 2002.

Mary Ann Liebert   "Epidemiology of HIV/AIDS in Developing Countries:
                          The Children," *AIDS Patient Care and STDs*, vol. 5, no. 4,
                          2001.

Stephen J. Lurie   "Do Patents Prevent Access to Drugs for HIV in Develop-
                          ing Countries?" *Journal of the American Medical Associa-
                          tion*, February 2002.

Donald G. McNeil   "A Continent at Risk," *New York Times Upfront*, May 14,
                          2001.

Alan Mozes   "HIV Risk a Question of Place as Well as People," *Reuters
                          Health*, September 2002.

Jim Nelson   "The AIDS Deniers," *Gentlemen's Quarterly*, September
                          2001.

Sabin Russell   "New Crusade to Lower AIDS Drug Costs: Africa's Needs
                          at Odds with Firms' Profit Motive," *San Francisco Chroni-
                          cle*, May 24, 1999.

Rachel Sacks   "Beyond Our Borders," *Body Positive*, March 1999.

Haroon Saloojee   "HIV Infection in Children," *British Medical Journal*,
and Avy Violari   September 2001.

David Satcher   "From the Surgeon General: The Global HIV/AIDS Epi-
                          demic," *Journal of the American Medical Association*, April
                          1999.

Michael Scotti   "Africa Is Different from a Poor American Neighbor-
                          hood," *Vital Speeches of the Day*, November 15, 2001.

Moises Selman,   "Problems Encountered in High-Level Research in
Rogelio Perez-Padilla,   Developing Countries," *Chest*, August 1998.
and Annie Pardo

Kasturi Sen and   "Global Health Status: Two Steps Forward, One Step
Ruth Bonita   Back," *Lancet*, August 2000.

Donald Shepard   "HIV/AIDS Epidemic Far Worse than Predicted," *Choices*,
                          March 2001.

Time   "Paying for AIDS Cocktails: Who Should Pick Up the Tab
                          for the Third World?" February 2001.

Wayne Turner   "AIDS Incorporated," *Washington Monthly*, April 2001.

Vaccine Weekly   "Agreements Set Vaccine on Fast Track to Developing
                          Countries," June 2000.

Philippe Van de Pere   "HIV Voluntary Counseling and Testing in Community
                          Health Services," *Lancet*, July 2000.

Index